How to
Keep Your Faith
When Losing Everything Else

Roger W. Swanson

Masterpiece Creations

Scripture references:
King James Bible

Songs by Mike Murdock:
used by express permission of
Dr. Mike Murdock
Win-Song Productions

Other songs:
Christian Copyright Licensing, Inc.
License #300101

Cover design by Rodney Bergeson

Published by
Masterpiece Creations
27450 481st Ave.
Canton, SD   57013
(605)743-5972

Printed in the United States of America
by Thomson-Shore, Inc.
7300 West Joy Road
Dexter, Michigan   48130

ISBN 1-96649-166-1

COMMENTS FROM FRIENDS

"I have walked with Roger through his "Job-like" experiences over the past several years. Through it all, Roger has stayed faithful to the Lord, optimistic in his outlook, never complaining, but always believing in the goodness of the Lord and the Lord's ability to see him through it. Today his faith continues to be strong. He has the confidence that, in Christ, he is victorious."
Pastor Ronald J. Traub
First Assembly of God
Sioux Falls, SD

"I have known the author of this book for 42 years. During that time, I have been awed by his tenacious faith in God, despite the storms of life which have beaten upon him, yet never conquered him. My friend Roger, is a shining example of God's sufficient grace applied to the life of the child of God. Your faith in the sovereignty of God will be renewed and strengthened as you read the pages of this inspirational book."
Bruce Talso
Minneapolis, MN

"Roger is a very optimistic person who has always majored on the bright side of life, even when circumstances dealt him hard blows. He has never been one to complain or burden others with his troubles, but has drawn inner strength from his faith in God."
Dwayne Pederson
Neighbor and friend
Worthing, SD

I met Roger as the result of reading the manuscript for this book. While reading it, I fell in love with the author's personality and heavenly attitude. His love for the Lord, for Scripture, and for the music of God, captured my interest, as did his intensely winning smile. I saw a man who had every reason to feel defeated, yet was unwavering in his devotion to the Lord. He just *knew* God was up to something good in his life.

Before long, love blossomed between us, and I was privileged to become his wife. As it says in Joel 2:25, the years the locust hath eaten, God will restore—and He certainly has. Life with Roger is incredibly wonderful. God is so good.
Joyce Swanson
Roger Swanson's wife

THANKS

Since this is the first book I authored, I had no idea just how much time and effort it would take to complete the project. I thank God for supernaturally directing me to Joyce, the special person who eventually became my wife and who expertly guided me through the myriad of steps and procedures of writing, organizing and editing this book. I deeply appreciate her tireless efforts and encouragement.
Roger W. Swanson

Dedicated to the memory of
Matthew Shawn Swanson

CONTENTS

INTRODUCTION

Life in general, and the people we encounter, can certainly be difficult and cruel at times. A single incident of pain, or a continuing saga of tough times, can occur without warning anytime in our lives. When it does, it is so difficult to know exactly how to cope, how to keep balance and perspective, how to successfully survive all of the chaos, and above all, how to keep faith in a loving, all-powerful God. Even if you lose everything else of value in life, it is imperative that you not forfeit your faith in God. If you lose that essential anchor, there is absolutely nothing left to keep you from sinking "under the circumstances" and completely despairing of living. Life can become totally overwhelming, with questions such as the following: What if God doesn't make sense at the moment? Will I ever smile again? How long will this pain last? Why can't life and people be fair? What did I do to deserve this? How can I ever trust someone again? We have to find our own responses to these and other major questions. In our pondering, it is easy to understand why we might seriously consider chucking everything formerly valued, and running off to a distant place where no one knows anything about us. Hopefully, we could then start life all over again, and the painful things from our past would be gone and forgotten.

However, reality quickly declares this thought to be a mirage, a fantasy, because nothing really changes that much, just because we change locations. The biggest problem of trying to run away from everything painful, including the people or experiences that hurt you and left you with scalded memories, is that you still have to take yourself with you when you go. That's usually where at least part of the problem originated and continues to be perpetuated. Therefore, running away from problems solves absolutely nothing, except to create greater frustration in the long run. Ultimately, we still need to deal with ourselves.

Many people could write great "how to" books on a variety of subjects, simply because they are great writers. They have thoroughly researched a particular subject, or they have a tremendous ability to identify and sympathize with others. However, *this* book has been authored by someone who has personally experienced, over a period of about twenty years, a lengthy series of trauma, tragedy, and tribulation that threatened to destroy his life, his testimony as a Christian, and his faith in God. Nevertheless, everything that the enemy, Satan, meant for evil, God eventually turned into good. This book is a saga of severe pain and devastating loss, but also a revelation of Divine assistance and miraculous restoration. As you read the story, you may weep, you may smile, or you may simply be glad that you haven't experienced some of the same tragic things the author experienced. However, you will also certainly rejoice as you note the great things that God *can* do in a person's life, when He is able to get in complete control of that person. After you finish reading this book, you may want to give it to someone currently going through a tough time. The message of this book could become a lifeline to help them survive their pain and loss, and could help steer them back onto solid footing so they can move on with coping, loving and living.

CHAPTER
1

MATT'S BEEN KILLED

I BURY MY SON

A phone call after midnight brought the chilling news that my eldest son had lost his life in a pickup accident. This book is dedicated to his memory. Matthew Shawn Swanson (July 10,1973-October 13, 1995) is one of my five children.

His first name, Matthew, means "God's gift," and his middle name, Shawn, means "God's gracious gift." His name was chosen carefully, as were the names of my other children. Because his life was taken so suddenly, my family and I needed to release him back to the Lord. Though we certainly wished we could have held onto him longer in this life, this was no option for us. As Job 1:21 declares, "… the Lord giveth, and the Lord taketh away. Blessed be the name of the Lord." Even in the midst of great tragedy and grief, it is not only possible, but also very important, to be thankful to God and to worship Him, regardless of our loss and pain. We chose the words, "He's not gone. He's just gone on ahead" for the headstone of his grave, because those words convey our confidence that we shall see him again in the not-too-distant future.

At the time of his death at age 22, Matthew was employed full-time as an occupational therapist with a health care provider in Lincoln, Nebraska. He was also classified as a full-time student at the University of Nebraska at Lincoln. He was a junior, majoring in the same field in which he was employed. Though he had just been home the weekend preceding his death, he impetuously decided to come home again that fateful day. He got off work early on Friday evening, so he could come home to camp and hunt over the weekend with one of his cousins at the farm. (This property was homesteaded by his great-great-grandfather Carl August Swanson in 1870, and has been in the family ever since.) Camping and hunting ranked pretty high on Matt's list of priorities. On the way home, he lost control of his brand-new, Chevrolet pickup on a curve on Interstate 29, just inside the South Dakota border, near Dakota Dunes. He was wearing his seatbelt, but he was killed instantly as his pickup rolled several times after he slid into the median. There remains much mystery regarding the events that precipitated the accident, since he was not a reckless, careless driver. Therefore, we have had to commit our many unanswered questions to God, and allow Him to give us His perfect peace, the kind that surpasses all human understanding.

One of the policemen who came to the door with the bad news the night of his death, happened to be one of my former students. Many years previously, I had taught him in seventh grade. Now, this was "one of my kids" bringing me sad information about "one of my kids." The news he brought produced the normal disbelief and shock that happens to all parents when the "worst of all nightmares" occurs, receiving the shocking news of a child's untimely death. I quickly fell to my knees in prayer. As I prayed intensely from a broken, heavy heart, I observed that the words of Scripture verses and gospel hymns started flowing into my heart and mind. My recovery from this major loss in my life has been achieved largely because of the Bible verses and songs that the Holy Spirit continually brings to my mind. Not only do these verses and songs produce inner comfort and peace, but they also build my faith and assure me that God is always in control of every circumstance. I will never be beyond His ability to intervene in my crisis experiences or to supply my desperate needs. Even when nothing seems to make sense to my human understanding, I know I can still trust God and allow Him free reign in my life, to work out his perfect plans, all in His time. Our God is an awesome God.

SPECIAL MEMORIES

I treasure many memories of Matthew in my heart, but I will share just a few of them. Matthew had served in the U. S. Army, while stationed at Fort Bliss, in El Paso, Texas. He had been honorably discharged in 1994. During his short life, he developed many interests, some of it made possible because of the part of the country where he spent his tenure in the Army. He loved sky diving, camping, hunting, fishing, mountain climbing, rock rappelling and bull riding. He enjoyed cooking for himself and friends, working on his computer, and keeping in touch with friends via E-mail. He managed to maintain, with great pride, his motorcycle and pickup, and still have time for country music and dance. Somehow, he still found time to socialize frequently and extensively with many friends and acquaintances of all ages. He was a confident and outgoing person, one who truly lived life to the fullest, almost as though he had a premonition that his time on earth would be very short. There were few challenges that he didn't at least attempt to handle with great enthusiasm.

I fondly recall the last phone visit I had with him just a few hours before his death. He had called me on my toll-free business line, as was his custom, and we covered a number of topics. I was surprised to hear from him that day, because he had already called me twice that week. Among the many things we discussed was the fact that he had been thinking about going into a cow/calf operation in partnership with his cousin on the family farm. We also discussed the wisdom of his purchasing a duplex, so that he could begin building his estate by owning rental property. He wanted to live in one of the units and rent out the other. By owning the duplex, he could finally have a hunting dog, another of his keen desires. This could have not been possible as long as he lived in a rental apartment. We covered a number of other topics, but our final words spoken to each other declared, "I love you." That was a pretty normal way for us to end all of our conversations with each other.

Matthew loved the challenge of tough projects. He enjoyed testing the limits, even when he knew there was some risk and danger involved. As a kid, he loved to climb as high as he could in the weeping willow tree in our back yard. He liked to jump his bike over ramps he built on the sidewalk, but none of them seemed quite high enough to him. He apparently didn't worry much about the possibility of crashing on the other side of the ramp. I wouldn't call him reckless, just adventuresome. Of my five children, he was the one who gave his mom and me our greatest challenge as parents. I think all parents should have at least one child like this to raise, especially during those times when they claim to have all of the answers for raising other people's children.

Whenever possible, Matthew loved to spend time at the family farm with his cousins. Though he was lovingly teased, initially, as being a "greenhorn," he quickly gained their respect, and proved to be an asset in helping with farm work when he could. While living in town during his childhood, he received very limited exposure to farm machinery, but during his teen years he quickly adapted, under the supervision of his cousins and uncle. His favorite attire quickly became blue jeans, with cowboy boots and shirt, and a black hat.

I vividly recall the look on Matthew's face the day he shot his first pheasant at age thirteen, as we walked together with a group of friends through a cornfield during pheasant hunting season. "I got him," he yelled with surprise and elation, as the bird plummeted to the ground and he raced to pick it up. He also got the privilege of helping clean it.

Another fond memory I have of Matthew occurred when I delivered a used, red, 4 x 4 Chevrolet step-side pickup to him at Fort Bliss in El Paso, Texas, during his tenure in the army there. He had called several weeks earlier to tell me he was ready to buy a pickup. His motorcycle was not quite as practical as he had thought it would be for all his transportation needs. Furthermore, the motorcycle was now nearly paid for. I looked at local car lots and found this special vehicle that I thought looked like a "Matt truck." I didn't give him many details about the pickup, but I told him I knew he'd like it. I wanted it to be a bit of a surprise when he finally saw it. He trusted my judgment, and blindly completed his purchase negotiations and financing with the dealer. Then I personally delivered the pickup to him in Texas. I knew I faced a hard, two-day drive, but I told him to expect me to arrive at the YMCA on base at approximately 4:00 PM the day before his twenty-first birthday. He knew me to be very punctual in keeping my appointments, so I knew he would be waiting for me at that time. Sure enough, I pulled into the parking lot at exactly 4:00 PM, and Matthew was sitting on his motorcycle, waiting for me. I'll never forget the look of delight on his face as he took his first look at his pickup. It turned out to be nearly an exact twin to a pickup his best buddy in the Army already owned. On Sunday, he took me with him to the Baptist church that he often attended with several of his friends. There he introduced me to others at the church he knew. Furthermore, I noticed he was carrying his Bible, just like almost everyone else was doing. It was a lively, friendly church. I was so proud of Matthew, and thankful that he was interested in growing in his relationship with God, by being involved in a good church.

I also have precious memories of Matthew's unique, warm personality. He loved to greet people with bone-crunching hugs. He provided me with a whole new dimension and appreciation for the importance of openly demonstrating affection for people. I had experienced very little of this open display of affection during my growing up years. I still often reflect on the memory of the last big hug I got from him, and the spoken words that we loved each other, as we parted the weekend before his death. The very first thought that ran through my mind, as we entered the hospital room the night of his death to view his battered body, was that I would never receive another one of those precious hugs from him on earth. I still miss those hugs very much, and have vowed to always give lots of hugs to those who are special to me. I look forward to getting many more hugs from Matthew someday when I get to heaven. Until then, when I spend time in prayer, I regularly ask God to give Matt a big hug for me, and to tell him I love him. I expect to see him again soon, when it is my turn to leave this earth.

A DAD'S GOAL

One of the major goals of a Christian dad's life is to do everything possible to insure that his kids love and serve the Lord with all of their hearts while on earth. Each child must make his own decision regarding accepting God's plan of salvation. There is no such thing as a "group plan" that *automatically* covers our children, just because *we* serve God. Thus, it is extremely important that our children accept the Lord as their personal Savior, and allow Him to be the Lord of their lives. Of all the things we could hope and plan for our children, this issue is the most critical one. The Bible tells us in Proverbs 22:6 to "train up a child in the way he should go, and when he is old, he will not depart from it." It also tells us that "All things work together for good to them that love God, to them who are the called according to his purpose." (Romans 8:28) The Scripture does *not* say that all things are *good*, only that they will eventually *turn out* for good. God is still in control of everything that happens to us, and He always has our best interests at heart. Nothing appearing bad to us can stay bad for long. It must eventually turn around into something good. That is God's promise to those who love Him and want His will for their lives. Though Matthew's life on earth has ended, I have full confidence and peace that he is now with the Lord. Therefore, my ultimate goal for him, that he spend eternity in Heaven, has already been achieved. What greater desire could I possibly have for Matt than this? Nothing that Matthew would experience on earth, if he were still alive, could possibly compare with what he is experiencing now. That is another example of something bad (Matt's death) that has turned out for good. I know where he is, and I know I will see him again someday soon.

I continue to pray daily for my other four children. I am thrilled to know that each of them has already made a personal salvation decision for the Lord, and I pray that each will maintain a vital, growing relationship with Him throughout their lifetime. As that occurs for them individually, I am filled with thanksgiving and praise to the Lord. How can a Christian dad measure his level of success as a dad, except in the manner he passes his spiritual values on to his kids? These values have meaning not only in this short life on earth, but also throughout eternity. If we *only* give our kids financial wealth and help them develop their natural talents, we severely impair them, since these material things are always subject to rust, theft, and corruption. Such things are a part of this transitory world. The measure of *true* wealth is counted in the lives of the people we influence for the Kingdom of God. The only treasures we can take with us from earth to heaven are *people*. Everything else stays here on earth, and has no lasting value, because all of these other things will eventually be destroyed. Our children must be able to observe a living demonstration in our own lives, of the things we truly consider of greatest value. What we *do* always speaks much more loudly than what we *say*. If our actions do not validate what we say, it automatically creates a credibility gap that is very difficult for our children to overcome.

As I stood by Matthew's casket the day of his funeral, and shared my grief and faith with the several hundred people in attendance, I challenged them to make sure they take advantage of every opportunity to hug those who are precious to them, while they still have the chance. There is nothing worse than coming to the end of life, and wishing things could have turned out much differently, especially in our personal relationships. I ended my remarks that day by saying, "Thank you, God, for the gift of Matthew for 22 years." I knew "good kids" were hard to come by, and God had blessed me mightily by giving me *five* of them.

A MOST UNEXPECTED ENCOUNTER

Our family experienced something very unusual and unexpected as the result of Matthew's death. The story is almost unbelievable. When I share it with most people, they often look at me totally speechless, or they have tears in their eyes.

Matthew was adopted into our family as a baby. We were not given much information about him or his birth parents. All we knew, for sure, was his given birth-name and the out-of-state town of his birth. As we had done with his older adopted sister, we shared the matter of adoption with him very early. Both of these kids knew they were "chosen kids." On numerous occasions, Matthew expressed sincere thankfulness to us for adopting him. Few people knew he and his sister were adopted, because we did not make an issue of the adoptions. Whether our kids were adopted or natural, they were still *our* kids. I was equally proud to be considered the father of *all* of them. They blended together very well as a family unit, and we tried to treat them as equally as possible, taking into account the differences in their temperaments.

After being notified of Matthew's accident, several of us journeyed to the hospital where he had been declared "dead on arrival." During the 90-mile trip, I sat in the back seat and quietly, prayerfully cried out to the Lord. I often just repeated the precious name of Jesus to myself. (I know what comfort just the mention of that special name brings to *all* believers in times of crisis, pain and loss.) Suddenly, I sensed an inner desire to find a way to get word to Mathew's birth parents about this tragedy. I had no idea *who* they were or *where* they were, but I felt they needed to be informed of his death, and also to know, from his dad's testimony, what a great, young man he had become. I did not share this thought with anyone else at that time, nor did I consider what a major undertaking this project could be. Just getting through the next several days of planning and having a funeral was going to take every bit of strength I could muster. I secretly determined to follow up on the matter later.

The day before Matthew's funeral, our family spent almost the entire day and evening at the funeral home. We did not want to leave Matthew's casket unattended, and we wanted to be together as a family. All of us wanted to organize our special memories for sharing publicly at the memorial service. Late that same afternoon, we observed two women enter the viewing room. We didn't know them, so we didn't approach them. They signed the guest book, spent a long time looking at the many pictures we had on display, and then spent some time at the open casket. As they got ready to leave, the younger one spoke to Matthew's mom and asked, "Are you his mom?" Upon receiving a positive nod, she handed her a sealed envelope, and the two visitors hurriedly left the room. We quickly tore the envelope open and read a letter containing information that left all of us in shock. The letter stated that the younger woman felt she might possibly be Matthew's birth mom. (Later I found out that she had contacted her adoption agency that same day, for some sort of confirmation before she came to the funeral home, but the agency was unwilling to assist her. Therefore, she felt compelled to take this giant risk of making some type of contact with our grieving family, uncertain of the impact it could have upon us, without any solid assurance that she was on the right track.) Her written declaration produced bewilderment in each of us, because we hadn't publicized the information, even at the funeral home, that Matthew was an adopted son. Certainly there had been no clue in the newspaper obituary to tip anyone off. It was just a brief story of a too brief life, and a family having to deal with the unexpected, tragic death of a precious son, an obituary story typical of many others that appear far too frequently in every newspaper.

My oldest daughter, Melissa, ran out after the two women and caught them just as they were getting into their car. They were seriously worried that we were going to be very angry with them for this intrusion into our grief, but they agreed to come back into the funeral home to meet with us. As we compared notes, everything checked out to satisfy us that she *was indeed* Matthew's birth mom, and the other woman was *her* mother. We spent precious moments hugging and weeping together, as each of us shared some of our special memories of Matthew with them. We invited them to attend the funeral service with us the following day, and they agreed to come. Little could I have known how God would work so miraculously, so quickly, in response to my prayerful desire the night of Matt's death, to find a way to get word of this tragedy to his birth parents. I hadn't given the matter any further thought, but God had seen fit to move in His typical, sovereign way, with or without my direct involvement.

Some time after the funeral, I had the opportunity to meet again with Matthew's birth mom to find out more about this very unusual set of circumstances. Our miraculous meeting the day before the funeral was obviously orchestrated by the Holy Spirit. There is no way it could have "just happened." His birth mom said that meeting our family, even under such tragic circumstances, and being able to attend the funeral with us, had brought about a spiritual rebirth in her own life. Ever since Matthew's birth, she had been plagued by the perpetual question as to whether she had done the right thing in giving him up for adoption. She told me that she gave birth to Matthew (Peter to her) when she was a high school teenager. During delivery, she was blindfolded and not allowed to touch him. He was taken away immediately after birth, and she was allowed no further contact of any kind with him. She eventually married and gave birth to two other children, but this "first-born" always remained very special in her heart. Only a mother can understand why it was so important for her to know he was doing well. She had no idea where he might be, but she was convinced that, if she ever happened to meet him somewhere, no one would need to introduce him to her. In spite of the fact that she had never seen him with her physical eyes, she knew that she would know him immediately. Again, only a mother can comprehend how this could be possible.

Interestingly enough, just two months prior to his death, Matthew's birth mom had come to the point where she desperately needed to bring closure to this matter. She hired a private detective to locate him, having no idea where he might be. Unfortunately, the detective had been overwhelmed with other cases, so he'd had little to get started on the project. She told me she had no intention of ever making personal contact with him. She just wanted to secretly find out where and how he was. She needed the full assurance that she had done the right thing in giving him up for adoption at birth.

The day the obituary appeared in the local newspaper, she picked it up and skimmed that section. As was her usual practice, she checked to see if she happened to know the deceased. As her eyes passed over Matthew's picture, his eyes seemed to lock onto hers. She paused to read further, and came to the date of his birth. Though we had listed our town as the place of his birth, because that is where he was born to our family, she was suddenly fully convinced that this had to be her birth child, the one she had never seen. For many years, both of our families had been living in the same town, and had never knowingly crossed paths. We discovered that her daughter had even graduated from high school with one of Matthew's younger sisters, and that her other son would eventually graduate with Matthew's younger brother. When she approached us at the funeral home, she was fully aware she was risking offending us in a major way, in case her presumptions were dead wrong. However, the approach she took that day was her only chance to get even a glimpse of the young man he had grown into. Furthermore, she was hoping there would be no family members present at the late afternoon hour when she visited the funeral home to view his body. Thus she would not have to make personal contact with us. Somehow the Holy Spirit had guided her and provided the courage and strength it took to boldly approach our grieving family the day before the funeral, to obtain the information she so desperately needed.

This incident clearly demonstrates the sovereignty of God. He has marvelous ability to control powerful circumstances in our lives, and to direct people into apparent chance encounters that end up forever changing our lives. In this case, He brought necessary healing to the broken heart of a mom who really needed to know that she had indeed done the right thing in giving up her newborn baby for adoption 22 years previously. He also brought the needed closure regarding her first-born. She now knew where he was, and that all was well with him. Furthermore, God miraculously answered my prayer the night of Matthew's death, regarding a sudden desire to get word to his birth parents about the tragedy. God chose a very unusual way to make it happen, and He didn't need my help to get the job done. God is a good God.

I want to include selected excerpts from a letter I received from Matthew's birth mom some time after our meeting. Her thoughts express the peace and faith God had provided to her. She wrote, "Thank you for your empathy and prayers...and thank you for your recent acceptance and friendship. Most of all, thank you for being the parent I could not be to Matthew. Matthew never belonged to me. He belonged to God. The miracle of finding him has been the 'experience of my lifetime.' I want you to know you have made all the difference for me by reaching out to me. You've taken away all the deep hurt I have felt...I am so glad you were a part of Matthew's life...how lucky Matthew was to be part of such a wonderful extended family. I will keep you in my prayers... I am a believer."

I'd like to share another heart-warming story associated with Matthew's death. It involves the son of one of

Mathew's cousins. A few months after his death, four-year-old David was riding with his aunt, Jennifer, as she drove from his home in Minnesota to the family farm in South Dakota. He kept her busy with a barrage of a wide variety of questions, typical of a four-year old. Then he asked suddenly this question, "Jenny, how did God get Matt out of that pickup when he died?" Jenny pondered this question for a bit and then responded that sometimes God uses angels to do things for Him. There followed a list of questions about what angels were. Finally after driving along in silence for a few miles, David suddenly announced, "I just saw Matt fly by!"

CHAPTER
2

CRISES, CHALLENGES AND CHANGES

IT HAPPENS TO US ALL

In my lifetime, which so far has spanned more than half a century, I have found that nearly every person alive, yes, even nearly every born-again child of God, *is* facing, *has* faced, or *will be* facing a crisis, a challenge, or a dilemma of some sort. Struggles, problems, and major challenges are quite common to all. It has been my personal observation that almost everyone experiences a struggle of some degree with their finances, marriage, career, physical or mental health, spiritual growth and maturity, children, or relationships with other people. Rarely are we without a need, a weak spot in our armor, or a serious dilemma. The "road of life" is filled with unexpected turns. Hopefully, no one is having a challenge or crisis in *all* of these common areas of struggle simultaneously, but it is easy to believe that many people are facing at least *one* of these at this very moment. Perhaps you are. If so, then this book is definitely for your encouragement and blessing, so keep reading. God wants to inspire you to "keep your faith" until you fully experience His total provision for your every need, no matter how desperate you might be.

People can easily get overwhelmed when the events of life pile up on them. That persistent need, that desperate dilemma, or that major emergency situation causes our focus to get fuzzy. We inevitably find that everything that can be shaken loose in our lives is quivering, and we find ourselves continually humiliated by our inability to get on top of the situation. Total victory seems just beyond our reach. It is never a fun experience to get "knocked up against the ropes" by the circumstances or calamities of life. However, when it *does* happen, we *must know* that *God will see us through* the experience successfully, and that *we will make it* to the other side. Yes, we *can* survive any crisis, no matter what it is, because *God will always come through* for us. I am convinced of this. This book contains the real life drama of how He certainly came through for me in every trial and testing I encountered.

RELIGION VS. RELATIONSHIP

When the serious questions of life or the storms of life begin to overwhelm us, we quickly find out whether we simply have "religion," or whether we have an active relationship with God to sustain us. Only an active, vibrant relationship with God will keep us steady, should everything else around us crumble and fall away. You see, religion is basically concerned with *head* knowledge, while a relationship with God is concerned with *heart* knowledge. Religion is primarily focused upon **d**octrines, **d**iscipline, **d**ogma, sundry **d**iscussions, and constant attempts to <u>d</u>o good things with our own strength and power. A relationship with God is based primarily upon establishing and maintaining a <u>r</u>ight standing (or relationship) by faith in Christ, experiencing the <u>r</u>eality of God's presence, knowing God's <u>r</u>ighteousness, maintaining <u>r</u>ight believing, following <u>r</u>ight living standards, and proving genuine <u>r</u>epentance by our speech and our actions, none of which can be accomplished with human effort or determination. It is accomplished from start to finish by faith alone in the provision of Christ. Religion represents the efforts of man trying to reach *up* to God, while a relationship with God simply reflects our response to God's reaching *down* to us. Religion puts emphasis on human efforts to attempt to gain God's favor and love by being "good enough." The emphasis is focused upon trying to lift ourselves by our own bootstraps to a level that will cause God to take positive notice of us, and at least be impressed with our sincerity, if nothing else. A relationship with God produces obedience and a positive response to His precious Holy Spirit. Thus, the Spirit of God and the Word of God are able to effectively administer grace and power to our lives and hearts. This is the only source that enables us to rise above all human understandings, strengths and abilities. That is why I re-iterate so confidently that only a relationship with God, through His Son, Jesus Christ, will ever enable us to keep our equilibrium when "all hell breaks loose" around us. A relationship with God will sustain us and provide a steady anchor, while "having religion" will only cajole, confuse, and condemn us. Anything less than a vibrant, personal, intimate relationship with God through Jesus Christ is not worth the powder it takes to blow it up. We may just as well discard it, because it has no true, lasting value, when we find the "chips are down," and we are experiencing a major crisis. We must have a faith that works consistently, a faith that will allow God's grace and power to flow *to* us and *through* us. When the storms of life and the powers of hell itself encircle us, and try to distract, diminish, delay, devour, destroy, or detour us, we must know that everything will eventually work out great for us. *Anyone* can smile and be happy when everything "comes up roses," and everything touched "turns to gold." It's *another* thing to smile when everything goes wrong and everything done appears to be "a day late and a dollar short."

The main reason I find religion, by itself, a total waste of time, is that it tends to give people a false sense of security. People who are religious tend to diligently follow certain rules and regulations. They are convinced God will accept them into heaven because the good things they've done will outweigh the bad things they've done. This idea is not scriptural, because Jesus made it very clear that, *except a man be born again* (John 3:3-5), he cannot enter the kingdom of God. There *must* be a spiritual birth, a specific time when they accept Christ as their *only* Savior. God does not have grandchildren. He only has children. We cannot have a relationship with God because of someone *else's* experience or relationship with God. We must have our *own* salvation experience, or we will end up in hell after this life is over.

LOSS AND GAIN

Have you ever felt you could identify with Job, the very rich man about whom the book of Job was written in the Old Testament? I have read that story many times over the years, and have felt I could easily empathize with the things Job was feeling because of numerous, nearly simultaneous tragedies in his life. Job was a very wealthy man, blessed of God in so many ways. He had many children, and he owned a lot of land and livestock. In fact, the Bible declares that he was the richest man in his part of the country. In anybody's book, these blessings would be valuable assets. Furthermore, he was a man who pleased God and spent time praying for his children. His life of diligence and sacrifice reaped marvelous benefits.

Suddenly, in the midst of all of this great blessing and prosperity, everything changed dramatically in a very short period of time for Job, as one bad report on the heels of another was delivered to him. Job could identify with the adage, "When it rains, it pours." In the course of just one day, Job was reduced to utter poverty, total despair, and tremendous physical pain. All ten of his children were killed when a tornadic wind destroyed the house where they were attending a party for one of their siblings. Then all of his livestock were either killed or stolen from him in a series of calamities. Finally, Job found himself covered with sores all over his body. Every symbol of his health and wealth were stripped from him one way or another, and Job lost everything that day, except his wife and his faith in God. Actually, at that point, his wife didn't prove to be much of an asset to him, either. She suggested that perhaps he should just "curse God and die." However, Job gently responded that she was speaking like a very foolish woman, and then he just bowed his head and worshipped God, even in the midst of all his pain. Worshipping God may seem to be a very *strange* thing for a person to do at a time like that, but it is definitely the *right* thing to do. Job's friends soon showed up to try to comfort him, but they were not able to be of much assistance to him. They were convinced that Job had sinned or offended God in some way (the only thing that perhaps ever makes any sense to the natural man), and much of the rest of the book of Job contains their sundry discussions as they try to unravel this strange set of circumstances.

Job did not find out until much later that all of these tragedies were not God's idea at all, but rather that they were orchestrated directly by Satan. God allowed it to happen, but Satan was the instigator. Thankfully, the story of Job ended with circumstances turning around completely for him. My favorite verses in the book of Job are 42:10-12, "And the Lord turned the captivity of Job when he prayed for his friends. And also the Lord gave Job twice as much as he had before…and the Lord blessed the latter end of Job more than the beginning." Job went through very difficult times, but God never abandoned him. In spite of overwhelming discouragement and despair, things changed dramatically for him when he began to pray for his *friends*, instead of just praying for *himself.* Apparently this was the real key to total recovery for Job. He got his focus *off* his own troubles and began to see the needs of *others*, instead. That is what got God's immediate attention and Divine response to Job's dilemma.

Most of us spend way too much of our prayer time praying for our *own* needs, rather than for the needs of others. Our prayer times are primarily spent praying items of petition for ourselves and our immediate families. We get so engrossed in our personal problems. Our typical prayer is, "God bless me and my wife, my son John and his wife, us four, no more." We completely overlook the fact that others around us are also facing crisis experiences in their lives. Thus, what happened in Job's life is an important lesson for us to learn as well. No matter how tough things get, we are never left alone in our pain and grief. God is always there to help us survive the crisis victoriously. Therefore, rather than camping beside our problems and wallowing in our misery, we must get up and start moving forward in faith toward total healing and recovery. We can best accomplish this by reaching out in love to others who are also in great present need. God responded to Job's prayer activity with unparalleled generosity and a new lease on life, because he acknowledged that God is always a *good* God, that all of his troubles originated only with Satan, and that he (Job) wasn't the only person alive who had a need. Furthermore, none of us can wait until *all* of our *own* needs are met before reaching out to minister to others in *their* need. Otherwise, for most of us, the time of ministry and blessing to others will *never* come. We will *never* get to that place and time in life when our own needs are *fully* met. God's way are so much higher than ours. Therefore, the way God often works in us will not, and cannot, make perfect sense to our human understanding. Occasionally, we must "act in faith" and pray on behalf of someone else's need *first,* before God does anything to address our own desperate personal need.

Regardless of where we are materially, physically, spiritually, emotionally or socially at any given time in this world, things can change quickly. All of a sudden, without warning, we can find ourselves in devastating circumstances, similar to those Job experienced. It is possible that, every time we begin feeling we are getting back on our feet, another bad report, another messenger bearing evil tidings knocks at our door, and we "hit the dirt" again, wondering what else can go wrong. As Christians, we acknowledge knowing the truth that God loves us, and we profess that we love Him. We even proclaim that we want to serve Him and please Him. However, when we look at others around us, it may appear that no one else is experiencing anywhere near the level of difficulties and pain that we are. What is wrong? What have we done to deserve this? Where is the "God of miracles" now when we need Him so desperately? Doesn't God care or know about what we are going through? Remember the truth Job discovered. The trials and the struggles that he experienced were not even God's idea. They came from Satan himself. Furthermore, God did not abandon Job in his dilemma, and God won't abandon you and me either. God has big plans for you and me, if we will respond to our troubles in the same manner Job responded to his.

WHY HAS ALL OF THIS HAPPENED?

There is another interesting person who experienced tough times, as described in the book of Judges, in the Old Testament. His experience can also help us maintain clear perspective during our own tough times. The sixth chapter of Judges records the story of an angel appearing to a man named Gideon one day. He was hiding in the woods, secretly threshing a meager supply of grain. An enemy army had conquered the land of Israel and stolen or destroyed their food supply. Gideon's family, like several others, had hidden some of their grain to help tide them through this tough time of famine, but their future looked bleak indeed. As the angel appeared that day, he greeted Gideon as a "mighty man of valor." That is hardly what anyone else would have said about this man who was hiding like a coward from the enemy. At the angel's greeting, Gideon's first response was, "IF GOD IS WITH ME, WHY HAS ALL OF THIS HAPPENED?"

That sounds like a pretty typical response that could come from any of us when things are going badly in our lives. When we hit tough times, it is so easy to presume that God must have abandoned us, that something is desperately wrong between God and us. Our human understanding can't see into the future to know how all of the current problems will be solved, and God usually isn't real good about giving us much advance information on what He is up to in our lives. That's because He wants our complete trust and faith. We wouldn't need Him and His help if we knew the complete story of what was really happening in our lives, and how it would eventually turn out.

The angel who came to Gideon could see into the future and see what great things God was going to do in and through him, while Gideon's entire focus was upon trying to scrounge enough food for his family to eat that day. He couldn't see the *big picture* that God could see. It's a good example of tunnel vision. It's logical for us to assume that, if God is *really* with us, then everything will always go smoothly for us. Therefore, we expect God to enable us to always be prosperous, in great health and in good humor. Occasionally I run into fellow Christians who believe, teach and attempt to practice this type of thinking. However, I have not observed most born-again believers personally experiencing this as a reality in their daily lives. It is a great idea, but it doesn't seem to compute into actual experience in the real world of human beings. The tough times *still* come to us. When they come, we must quickly decide whether we will continue trusting God for His answers, deliverance, and provision, or whether we will just go off somewhere and have a major "pity party" for ourselves. If we do the latter, we are simply declaring that God's Word can't be trusted and that God is a liar. That reaction severely impacts God's ability to help us.

God *never* promised His children that the circumstances of this life would always be fair. He *didn't* promise other people would always treat us properly. He *didn't* say we would always feel able to cope with the circumstances of life, or always feel great or happy. He didn't even promise we wouldn't make dumb mistakes on our own. However, God *did promise His grace would always be sufficient* (II Corinthians 12:9) and God *did promise He would never leave us nor forsake us* (Matthew 28:20). Those promises help us maintain balance and proper perspective.

I have had multiple traumatic experiences over the past few years. Many times I thought I received much more than my fair share of them. Nevertheless, in spite of them, *I have definitely known the ongoing, sufficient and sustaining grace of God in my life.* That is why I feel compelled to share, from my personal, intimate and embarrassing experiences, important concepts of how to hang onto God, or more properly put, how to allow Him to hang onto me. I certainly found that God kept me safe and secure during those times when it seemed I was losing everything I considered worthwhile in this life. I sincerely trust that the Scriptures, thoughts and songs which the Holy Spirit consistently brought to *my* heart and mind to help me during those difficult times, will also provide encouragement and blessing to *you.* Perhaps you might be thinking right now that *all hope is lost. There is no more time. It is all over for me. Even God must be looking the other way.* If so, I have *great news* to share with you. Your Source is still the Lord God almighty.

I have also come to realize that, just because someone is smiling on the outside, doesn't necessarily mean he isn't crying on the inside. It is not easy to share all of the intimate details of personal grief, pain or embarrassment with other people. It is so much easier to try to bury the pain and pretend everything is just fine. However, that is *not* how God would have us act. We are *not* to act like an ostrich, which buries its head in the sand when trouble comes. God wants us to be genuine examples to the world, of how people of faith can keep their eyes focused upon Jesus, regardless of what is happening to them. He is the author and finisher of our faith. No matter *what* is going wrong, no matter *what* the doctor's report says, no matter *what* cruel thing someone else said or did, no matter *what* stupid thing we ourselves might have done, Jesus *knows, cares, and is able to help us cope with it all.* This world we live in contains many unexpected turns in the road, and God wants us to come through each and every experience, knowing that *He* has seen us safely through the tough times, as well as the good times. He will *always* provide us with His Divine strength, wisdom, and ability. Then we will be better able to personally testify of *God's* greatness, and better able to reach out to encourage others experiencing the throes of despair, discouragement, testing, or loss. Our smiles need not be fake "put-ons." Rather, they can be the result of the true "Joy of the Lord" flowing in our lives because we have found, from first-hand experience, that God is *still* on the throne, and that He really *does* have everything under control.

What follows, then, is a chronicle of my personal testimony of God's faithfulness and sustaining grace. I *know* that it is real, that it really *does* work, even in the time of great, overwhelming tribulation. I *know* of a certainty, that I *can* make it, and that God *does* indeed keep His promises to His children. I know this for a fact, because it happened, and is continuing to happen for me. Therefore, this is a story, *not* so much about me, but rather about the *love, grace and power of God,* which He has manifested and demonstrated to me.

As I previously mentioned, the Holy Spirit often brings the words of Scriptures or Gospel songs to my mind. These words continually bring renewed faith and encouragement to me during the tough times I experience. The Word of God and the music of God are both powerful forces that enable God's children to "hang on til the miracle comes." They speak mightily to the inner man, to build faith and assurance.

> *Let the word of Christ dwell in you richly*
> *in all wisdom; teaching and admonishing*
> *in psalms and hymns and spiritual songs,*
> *singing with grace in your hearts to the*
> *Lord. Colossians 3:16*

Throughout this book, I demonstrate the importance of the Word of God and the music of God, by including many illustrations of each. As an example, I include this song, because it speaks of such foundational truth and understanding.

I MUST TELL JESUS
Elisha A. Hoffman (public domain)

I must tell Jesus all of my trials,
I cannot bear these burdens alone.
In my distress He kindly will help me.
He ever loves and cares for His own.

I must tell Jesus all of my troubles.
He is a kind, compassionate friend.
If I but ask Him, He will deliver,
Make of my troubles quickly an end.

Tempted and tried, I need a great Savior,
One who can help my burdens to bear.
I must tell Jesus, I must tell Jesus,
He all my cares and sorrows will share.

O how the world to evil allures me.
O how my heart is tempted to sin.

I must tell Jesus, and He will help me
Over the world the vict'ry to win.

Chorus—
I must tell Jesus. I must tell Jesus.
I cannot bear my burdens alone.
I must tell Jesus. I must tell Jesus.
Jesus can help me, Jesus alone.

CHAPTER
3

WHAT *ELSE* CAN GO WRONG?

At one point in my life, I was well on my way toward becoming a millionaire. At least things looked real good on paper. I thought becoming a millionaire was a very worthwhile goal at the time, and I *still* don't think there is anything wrong with becoming one. However, my personal goals have modified considerably, after experiencing a series of major calamities and set backs over a seemingly endless period of years.

After I graduated from college, I taught school for four years. I taught seventh grade language arts and social studies, and thoroughly enjoyed my job. At that time, I fully expected to teach for the rest of my life. I even began working on my Master's degree one summer at the University of South Dakota. The following year, I determined to complete that graduate degree as quickly as possible, so I arranged a year's leave of absence from my teaching position. However, that specific plan got interrupted during the summer months before I started classes, because I decided to marry the very special girl I had been dating off and on for several years. By the time I made that decision to marry her, my teaching position had already been filled for the coming year, so I was faced with the immediate need to find another way to make a living. Therefore, I became a "teacher dropout," without actually intending to be.

I started selling life and health insurance. After a short time of that, I also obtained my real estate license, thus beginning a challenging career in sales for which I feel I was divinely destined. I still use the education gained from my teaching years. Many of the teaching techniques are utilized in my real estate business, and I approach the business more as a counselor than a salesman. It is my job to represent people and provide information that helps solve their real estate problems. It is up to *them* to take the information and make the final decision about what's in their best interest. I don't try to talk them into making decisions, as a typical salesman would. God has richly blessed me in the real estate business for over 28 years. My job has provided a daily experience of walking by faith, because I have needed to depend greatly upon the Lord for His help in being productive and successful in reaching my goals. A career in sales can be both challenging and fulfilling, and I always look forward to getting up each morning and heading for the office, to experience whatever God is going to do *with* me and *through* me that day.

During this time of beginning a new career, I read numerous books about positive thinking, and "how to" books on setting and achieving financial and personal goals. The basic idea was, if I didn't know where I was going, I wouldn't know when I arrived, or I'd end up somewhere else. The importance of always maintaining a good positive mental attitude was drilled into my mind. Since I was already a natural optimist, I quickly absorbed these ideas and concepts into my subconscious, and began working diligently toward the achievement of the many new goals I set for my life and business. I had become a born-again Christian, with a personal assurance of eternal salvation, at an early age, so I had a genuine desire to serve God and to please Him with my life. When I was in public high school, several of my classmates referred to me as "preacher" because I often carried my Bible with my textbooks. However, in looking back over the events which eventually occurred in my life, I can see clearly that a lot of my goals were really just that—*my* goals!

In due season, my financial acquisitions included a part-interest in 160 acres of good South Dakota farm land, and I owned and managed a number of income-producing rental properties. The people I was using as my role models, and the books that I read, gave me a good understanding about the concept of leveraging my equity positions. This made it possible to acquire additional property more quickly, using wrap-a-round or blanket-type mortgages, so that all of my net asset equity was engaged in working for me to rapidly build my estate. I was amazed at how much property I quickly acquired. My wife and I eventually purchased a lovely, four-bedroom, Dutch Colonial home for our family in the "right" part of our town. We then filled it with expensive furniture. It was not uncommon for me to purchase two new cars a year, so that my wife and I could each drive one.

My business was prospering, and I soon acquired a 23' GMC front-wheel drive motorhome equipped with a

---

mobile phone. I used this vehicle as a mobile office for my real estate business. As pretentious as it may have appeared, it was very effective and quite practical for regular, daily use. It also provided some excellent income tax deductions. Since this took place in 1978, and I was the first Realtor in my city to use a motorhome in this manner, my public image as one of the top-producing real estate agents was greatly enhanced. Eventually, there were four or five other agents who followed suit, until the Arab Oil Embargo took place and the price of gas rapidly escalated. I responded quickly, and downsized to a conversion van.

In addition to all this, I had a part-interest in an airplane, and was working on my private pilot's license. If something desirable was out there and could be financed, I tried to find a way to make it happen for me. Life was very good for me, and anyone who casually observed me at that time would most likely have thought I was a guy who was really going places, a person who was a true model of success. My future appeared to be very rosy.

Getting credit from lending institutions in those days was quite easy. I was on my way toward rapidly fulfilling my surging goals, by legally using "other people's money," and aggressively leveraging my progress to the "top of the financial heap" at a relatively young age. I was trying to follow the suggestions of the financial wizards who wrote the books I was reading. I was also inspired by the legend of my paternal grandfather, who successfully survived the Great Depression of the 1930s and became a very wealthy man, through the acquisition of an impressive number of farms. I recalled a statement credited to Will Rogers who said, "Buy land, they ain't making any more of the stuff."

I acknowledge that the value of my fantastic wife and five great kids was somewhat overshadowed by my dogged determination for financial attainments. I realize now that I took my family for granted at times. I was not the perfect husband or father much of the time, because of all the other distractions going on in my life. Nevertheless, my family was always very special to me, and I was very proud of them. I still am.

Little did I know, at that time, that I had inadvertently "painted myself into a corner" with my lifestyle and my overly positive outlook on life. I was about to experience many events, beyond my control, which quickly unraveled all of my wonderful goals and plans. The national economy experienced a severe decline, better known as the "Carter years." None of those books I had been reading prepared me for all the pain, stress, struggle, and loss that was about to transpire in my life. I don't recall reading very much about building a cash cushion, or about how to arrange one's finances so that one could better survive tough financial circumstances. Instead, I felt like a "toad batting his eyes in a hail storm," as a seemingly endless saga of major setbacks occurred in my life. Over and over, I was faced with multiple obstacles, to the point that I began to wonder if life could ever again return to normal. In fact, I lost touch with what normal was. Earlier on, I knew, from personal experience, how it felt to provide assistance, encouragement and advice to *other* people who are going through tough times. Later I learned

---

how differently it felt to have tough times happening to *me*.

How *does* a person cope? Where *does* a person go for help and advice? What *should* one do next? Who has the *right* answers? Who can one *trust* or *confide in* while struggling to get back on one's feet? Does *anyone* have any idea of what's really happening? Is there *anyone* who really cares?

The multiplicity of questions can easily overshadow the right or proper answers. It is so easy to be overwhelmed with feelings of paranoia, despair, discouragement, and even depression. It is almost impossible to maintain a proper perspective or focus, when problems come in such rapid sequence that they seem to create a "domino-effect" in one's life. There is no easy way out of the mess. Pleading temporary insanity doesn't cut it. Even bankruptcy doesn't cure anything, except to perhaps give a brief respite to catch one's breath and get focused again. I refused to seriously consider that alternative, so I was left with only one choice. I had to take one day at a time, one step at a time, and hope for the best, trusting that my creditors would be patient with me.

In this chapter, I will summarize some of the major crises I encountered in seemingly rapid succession, some even simultaneously. I will address the dilemmas I faced, which altogether span a period of about twenty years of my life. Perhaps you can identify with one or more of them. In the final chapter of this book, I will share with you how God worked mightily in me over that period of time to meet my overwhelming needs, providing healing and restoration to me in each situation.

CANCER

First of all, I had to deal with cancer in my immediate family. My mom was diagnosed with breast cancer at the age of 61. The doctors wanted to operate and hopefully keep her alive a few more years. However, she was convinced the Lord would heal her without an operation. The Lord had *already* healed her of the same condition a few years previously, and she had been getting along very well, until this new episode flared up. This was a very difficult time for our family, as we watched her slowly get worse instead of better. After a brief stay in the hospital, she insisted on going home, where she had lived since her marriage nearly 40 years earlier. Eventually, she needed an oxygen tank standing by, to assist her with breathing. Many people were praying for her and believing God for a miracle to spare her life.

One day, as I drove back from visiting Mom at the farm, I spent my driving time praying for her. Through my tears I heard myself pray, "Lord, if you are *not* going to heal her in this life, please just take her home quickly, so she doesn't have to suffer like this anymore." That same afternoon, just a few days before Christmas, my mom asked Dad for his assistance, so she could get up from her recliner and stand in front of the big windows that looked out over the farm. Dad later told me that she stood there for awhile in her weakened condition, and lifted her voice in audible praise and worship to her Lord. This was a favorite activity of hers. (I remember so well, while still living at home, hearing her audibly praise the Lord and sing, while doing her household chores. She maintained a very vital, daily relationship with the Lord, through her Bible reading, prayer, and worship. That was a powerful example to me while I was growing up.) After standing there a short while, she asked Dad for his help in getting to the bed in the other room. As he gently laid her down, she looked up at him, told him that she loved him, and then closed her eyes in death. She received her total healing that day, but not quite the way she thought she would. You see, there is no more cancer in the world that she entered. What a way to go! I can't imagine a greater way to leave this physical life behind than by falling asleep in Jesus, right after telling your lifetime mate that you love him.

TAKING UP THE CHALLENGE

An additional pressure in my life occurred because of my involvement in helping start a Christian television station in our community. I was part of a team of local businessmen who originally incorporated the ministry of Team TV when it signed on the air in 1978. Almost immediately, the operation got into serious financial straits, and the initial nest egg began to melt "like butter on a hot stove," with out-of-control expenses. The challenge we had been given by our local cable system was an unbelievable opportunity, and we were convinced the Lord was specifically leading us. In spite of this, we were quickly heading for corporate bankruptcy. The board responded decisively by requesting the resignation of the designated, paid management. Then they asked me to volunteer my time, to see if I could get things back on track and salvage the operation. Eventually, all of the other board members resigned to focus on other interests. With the help of God, and a few very dedicated supporters, I was left to do my best to keep the ministry alive. This additional crisis came at a very inopportune time in my life. So many major distractions in my personal life were beginning to occur, and they were already on the "front-burner" of my attention focus. This is a miracle story of God's faithfulness, and I will share the complete story in chapter seven.

"NO MON-NO FUN"

Because of what was happening in the national economy, real estate sales slowed down dramatically. Long-term interest rates, for mortgages used to finance the properties I was selling, soon escalated to over sixteen per cent. (I earn my living as an independent contractor, which means my income is based solely on commissions received when new owners take possession of a home after the closing takes place. No salaried income or draw, fringe benefits, retirement or insurance benefits are provided.) Because of the slowdown in sales, my commission checks got spaced further and further apart. When my commission checks sometimes became spaced several months apart, all attempts at budgeting became just a bad joke. I've never found anyone who could come up with a good way to make a budget work when there is no certainty about how much income is coming, or when it is expected, especially if the next expected check may still be several weeks or months away. Initially, I was able to borrow money to temporarily hold my financial world together, by utilizing some of my paper equity as collateral, hoping the economy would quickly turn around. However, the interest rate for that type of borrowing soon catapulted to twenty-two per cent, making it a short-lived solution. Everyone knows it is impossible to live very long on borrowed money. Those former days of easy credit quickly vaporized, as the reality of a looming personal, major crisis began to unfold.

PAPER WEALTH

The feelings of loss and hopelessness compounded when, one by one over a period of time, all the properties in my recently-acquired portfolio were either sold at big discounts, or were foreclosed by the lender because I couldn't hang unto them any longer. At this point, the market values were nowhere near what I paid for them, or even what I owed against them. I discovered how quickly "wealth on paper" evaporates when a period of rapid inflation in values follows a period of readjustment, as the economists call it. There was a lot of negative publicity circulating about me in the community, because my name was frequently appearing in the legal section of the local newspaper as the result of actions being taken against me by creditors. I wondered what in the world was happening to "this rising star in real estate." In spite of this loss of face, I struggled desperately to salvage what possessions I could, though I was willing to let them *all* go, if necessary. I feverishly tried to figure out a magical formula to preserve at least a *portion* of my self-respect and good reputation. One thing was sure. Though bankruptcy was recommended, I didn't want any part of it. I had created the debt in good faith, and I intended to do everything in my power to make things right with the people who had trusted me.

EMPTY PANTRY

Over the next few years, there were several times when I came home to find that another utility company had disconnected one of our services that day. Thus, our dream home was now without heat, lights, phone, or water. My pattern of untimely payment wasn't taken lightly by the utility companies. I assure you it wasn't easy to explain to my family why we were having such a struggle, when all of our friends were experiencing no such dilemma. How could I look my kids in the eye and give them a rational explanation as to why the grocery pantry was empty again, and why I wasn't sure when the next check would come so it could be replenished? Macaroni and cheese, or mashed potatoes and wieners for every meal sure got old in a hurry. How could I seriously expect to remain active in the real estate business, when a major part of my business was generated via the phone, and any potential customers trying to make contact with me were occasionally given a cryptic message that my phone has been disconnected? What could I do when the gas tank was empty again? I hated to ask the kids to break their piggy banks to find a couple more dollars to tease the car into going a few more miles before sputtering again?

CHAPTER THREE

NO WHEELS

One day a tow truck arrived to tow my best car away. Obviously, the bank got tired of waiting for expected payments they never received, because of uncontrollable delays in receiving my commission checks on pending business. I was uncomfortable telling potential clients that they needed to meet me at the office so I could ride with them in their car to see properties. Most Realtors can't be successful in their business without a car, and most of them drive decent-looking ones. This put me in an extremely difficult position. At one point, I was fortunate enough to borrow a farm pickup from one of my uncles for a couple of months, until I was able to talk another car dealer into taking a chance on me. At other times, my only option was to drive some pretty rough-looking, older model cars, vehicles originally acquired for one of the kids to drive. This option was a pretty difficult pill for me to swallow, especially when I love nice cars as much as I do.

EVICTED

It is difficult to describe the hopelessness I felt when I received an eviction notice from the bank holding the third mortgage on our family's dream home. The redemption period following the sheriff's sale had expired several weeks earlier. Praying for another miracle at this point was not going to gain any more leniency, and everything else I had tried to do, either to sell or refinance the home, had come to no avail. I didn't know where to begin looking for suitable replacement housing, because I had a family of seven people and two dogs. I knew I couldn't promise the next landlord or bank that things would actually get any better for me. How could I explain to my kids that everything would have to go into a storage unit, and that we would be living for several weeks in two adjoining rooms of a local motel until we could get into another house again? Two meals a day were fixed with a microwave oven and a camp refrigerator. That experience certainly brought our family "closer together" in a way we had never considered. At a time like that, we really appreciated the value of having true friends who came alongside and helped with the moving project. I was also deeply grateful for the generosity of a couple of my uncles who provided a loan to help us get into another home, using some very creative financing.

LEAVING OUR CHURCH

In addition to the pressure of relocating my family that year, I encountered another major crisis. I struggled long and hard over the eventual conclusion that we could no longer remain a part of the particular church where we had been heavily involved most of my adult life. A new pastor had recently come. Because of his attitude and actions, he ended up driving family after family away from the church. Many people were severely hurt, emotionally and spiritually, by this situation, and some have not fully recovered to this day. I earnestly sought God's face in prayer for wisdom and discernment in dealing with this dilemma. I waited patiently for an answer, while the situation continued to only grow worse over a period of time. Though I was a member of the board, I soon realized the hopelessness of my making any further significant difference with my influence. I came to the important realization that it was *God's* church, not mine. Therefore, God was fully capable of taking care of these dear people in this congregation, and accomplishing whatever He wanted to perform regarding this pastor and his leadership techniques. The only remaining logical solution was for *me* to resign my positions of leadership in the church, and to take my family to another church in the community. I was determined that my children not become disenchanted by the things or the people of God, because of the kind of unspiritual actions or attitudes being displayed around them at that time. We decisively made the move, and have remained heavily involved at the new church ever since. This turned out to be a very beneficial decision, especially for my family, which demonstrates again how God can turn every bad situation into a good one, all in His time.

SHOPLIFTING

Shortly after moving my family to this new church, I received a phone call during choir practice one Sunday evening. I was informed that one of my sons had just been arrested for shoplifting. I made a quick trip to the store and confirmed that this was an unfortunate, but true situation. I met my son in the store office with the manager and a policeman. I struggled to understand what in the world would ever possess him to do such a ridiculous thing. Fortunately, he was released into my custody, upon our promise to meet with one of the detectives at the police station the following week. I accompanied him to this scheduled meeting. After a heavy discussion, he promised to commit no further offenses of this kind, so these "first offense" charges were dismissed. We had to deal with all of the normal feelings of personal embarrassment, as well as severely strained family relations, but the matter was never made public. Obviously I was not very proud of him at this point, but I still needed to let him know that I loved him, not because of *what he did*, but rather because of *who he was*. He was *my son*. Therefore, he received my unconditional love, though it was a form of "tough love." That is the same kind of love that God has demonstrated to me. He loves me *in spite of* all the stupid things I have done, and it was extremely important that I demonstrate this same kind of love to my son at that time.

Somehow we got through this difficult time together, and the matter of shoplifting was never discussed or repeated again. I firmly oppose the idea that parents bail their kids out of problems when they occasionally break various rules or even civil law. Neither should parents try to convince teachers or other authority figures that their children "couldn't possibly be guilty of committing the offense they are charged with." Too many parents prefer to portray their children as being completely innocent. These parents believe the real problem must originate with the authorities, certainly not with their darling kids. However, *all* children need to be taught to take full responsibility for their actions, no matter *what* their age. Otherwise, they won't develop into valuable assets to society, or even know a necessary level of success and achievement for themselves. It is certainly important to protect our children to the best of our abilities, but they must not be *over*protected.

A CRASHING WORLD

I have occasionally experienced the trauma of having a constable or sheriff deliver an official notice of a garnishment or judgment filed against me. All I could do was shake my head in despair, because I was helpless to forestall it. My circumstances had become like a snowball rolling downhill, as the financial crisis gathered momentum and magnitude. All past performances of paying my bills in a somewhat timely manner were shoved aside, as creditor after creditor jockeyed for the best position to attach what few assets remained. When another notice of "attempted delivery" appeared in my mailbox, informing me that a registered letter was waiting for me at the post office, it became so much easier to pretend I didn't get the notice. I didn't want to focus on who else might be trying to sue me. I have not seen many books on handling this kind of pressure, while maintaining sanity, balance, and good humor.

IT'S ALL MY FAULT

I found myself withdrawing into a private world of despair, but also into desperate prayer to the Lord, to help me resolve these issues. Meanwhile, there was little teamwork between my wife and me. We didn't work together to resolve these challenging matters. She told me that, "since I had gotten us into this mess, I needed to get us out of it." I fully admit that I made most of the financial decisions, without consulting her first. Today, I realize how totally stupid that was. I worked as hard as I could at my job of selling real estate, but, with so many distractions going on in my private life, I had difficulty keeping my mind on my work. It seemed that as soon as I got one problem solved, two more appeared. Getting my feet back onto solid financial ground was a very slow process. The pressure was still strong to take the easy way out by filing bankruptcy. I continued resisting this, convinced I had to find a better alternative. Nevertheless, I could not prevent us from eventually being evicted from this replacement home as well, several years later. We then moved to a rental home, and couldn't keep the rent paid in a consistent manner there either. Irregular income, coupled with the financial needs of a growing family of five children, while I was still saddled with monstrous debts to try to repay, certainly kept life in turmoil.

I DON'T LOVE YOU

The stress in my life reached a new pinnacle, when my marriage mate of nearly twenty-three years suddenly informed me that she had had more than enough of this seemingly-endless saga of pain and struggle. She told me that she didn't love me anymore, and that perhaps she never had. She was fully convinced she would be better off without me. The insecurity created by the forced loss of two homes that she dearly loved and had decorated to her special taste, was overpowering. She had lost faith in my judgment, as well as my ability, to ever get the family back onto solid financial footing. She had already taken official steps, privately, to file for divorce. I struggled to accept that as a rational option to our dilemma. I thought we both agreed that marriage was for life, and that divorce was *never* an option ever seriously considered by born-again Christians. How could this possibly be justified as God's will for us, or for her and the children? There must be far better ways to resolve the myriad of problems that occur in almost everyone's life. What did "until death do us part" really mean in our wedding vows? I was *very* opposed to the divorce, and she readily admitted knowing I still loved her, regardless of her plans for the divorce.

Because of the strain that our financial straits had put on our marriage for so long, my wife had previously determined, after the birth of our last child, that she would not allow any further physical activity to take place between us. Though we continued sleeping in the same bed, I was not allowed to kiss or touch her in any way. By the time she filed for divorce, this had gone on for a period of seven years. Regardless of how difficult this was for me to deal with, I was determined to do everything I could to try to make the marriage, and our finances, work. I continued to demonstrate total commitment and loyalty to her, but she withdrew from me, and we were no longer a team, working together to solve our difficulties. I am convinced that her decision of forced celibacy and lack of physical contact set the stage for the eventual divorce. Closing the door to intimacy of every kind prevents any serious level of communication from *ever* occurring in a marriage. Complicated situations occur in most marriages. Unless both the husband and wife work together to resolve the issues, the marriage dies internally, though things might still appear fine for a time, externally. Most of our friends had no idea that our relationship had deteriorated to the level of a brother and sister, rather than that of a husband and wife. We still treated each other civilly, but there was no romance left in our marriage. We had become as strangers to each other. Because she worked nights, a time when I could be home with the kids, and I worked days and many weekends selling real estate, we rarely saw each other, except when we went to church together.

Now my wife said that there was no turning back. I couldn't stop her from proceeding with the divorce. She gave absolutely no consideration to outside counseling, nor would she allow any opportunity, under any circumstance, for possible reconciliation. The marriage was *over!* She informed me that she and the kids were moving to another home, and I would need to find a more affordable place to live by myself. I then realized that it normally takes two people to fall in love and get married, but it only takes one to determine to end the marriage. Once that determination has been made, the other person is usually totally helpless to stop the procedure.

The pain and rejection of this divorce was, by far, the greatest setback I faced. Fortunately, the divorce was as amicable as it could possibly be. I could see no value in trying to contest it, and I also hoped that, in time, there could possibly be reconciliation of some kind between us, though I was the only one thinking that way. I was still allowed frequent contact with our kids. In fact, when she continued to work nights, I often stayed at her house with the kids, until she got off work at midnight. Then I returned to wherever I was living at the time. That opportunity allowed me to maintain some degree of positive relationship with my kids. In fact, my ex-wife eventually complemented me, saying she thought I became a better dad after the divorce, than I was before. Because I was hoping for an eventual reconciliation, I continued to wear my wedding ring for three years after the divorce. I jokingly told my kids that I did this because I didn't want other women to pester me, but I still couldn't fully accept the fact that our 23-year marriage was *really* over.

DAD, CAN I BORROW YOUR CAR?

Sometime after the divorce, and after a trying period of having to drive old, junky-looking cars, I was finally able to acquire a vehicle I highly-prized. It was a late model Nissan Maxima, equipped with all of the special features I loved. It was soon after this that my son came home on leave from the military, and asked to borrow my car so he could visit some friends. How could I possibly tell him that he couldn't borrow it? I simply gave him the keys and told him to be home early. However, he didn't come home by the time I went to bed. He awakened me the next morning to inform me that there had been a slight accident. I was decidedly heartbroken. There was nearly $2,000 in damage, and the story he told didn't quite make sense. What could I do? Would it really help if I put my fist through a wall, screamed or hollered? I didn't do *all* of these things, but they did seem appropriate to me at the time. We had a very unpleasant conversation in the parking lot of a local fast-food restaurant, which is not one of my favorite memories. The matter was resolved with him agreeing to pay the deductible on my insurance policy, so the car could be repaired. The insurance company paid the rest. The important thing I learned from this experience, is that absolutely *no* possession in this life should be allowed to have such a priority in our lives, that we allow relationships with our loved ones to be destroyed or overshadowed.

HEIDI IS GONE

A completely different kind of challenge occurred one sunny, Saturday afternoon. I was home with my seven-year-old daughter, when we experienced a crisis with our dog, Heidi. She was the family's registered Sheltie, and a very prized member of the household. While we were playing together in the backyard, a number of hot-air balloons took off from a nearby park. They flew low, right over our house. We stood and watched them awhile, and suddenly realized that Heidi was not around any longer. We called and called for her, but there was no response or sign of her anywhere. We realized that if we couldn't find her, we both would be in serious trouble with the rest of the family that evening. We certainly didn't need another major crisis in the family at this point in our lives. How the Lord met this crisis is also dealt with in the final chapter of this book.

DAD, I'M PREGNANT

Another very unexpected dilemma occurred when I received a call one evening from my single, college-aged daughter, informing me she was pregnant. After the shock wore off, I decided not to be unduly concerned about what the relatives, friends, and others might think and say about this new development. Instead, I gave prayerful consideration to providing her much-needed encouragement, unconditional love and support. She needed to make that all-important decision about whether to raise the child alone as a single mom, or to give it up for adoption. The baby's father didn't care which decision she made, because he had no interest in being further involved with either the child or her. Abortion was absolutely not considered, because, for many years, this particular daughter had been actively promoting the benefits of adoption over abortion. Though she was in the minority with her friends, she fearlessly declared abortion to be wrong in *all* situations. As a high school student, she even made a trip to the state capitol to speak to the state legislators during their session. She wanted to enlist their support for a bill that would encourage adoptions instead of abortions. You see, she was speaking from experience, because *she* had been adopted, instead of aborted. In the final chapter, I will share the outcome of this episode with you.

OH... THE PAIN!

One spring day, while driving home from an out-of-town appointment, I suddenly felt a severe, gut-wrenching pain in my lower abdomen. Every mile I drove seemed to bring an increase to my pain and discomfort. I seriously considered using the car phone to request an ambulance to meet me on the interstate highway. I knew that the pain couldn't be an appendicitis attack, because I had an appendectomy as a teenager. It seemed like I was hitting every red light in town, as I sped my way toward the nearest hospital. I will never forget the difficulty I had after I arrived, struggling to get out of the car and into the emergency room. I was sure I was about to die from the pain, before they got me admitted and escorted to the proper area. The eventual diagnosis was a kidney stone attack. Later I was told that this pain is similar in intensity to that of giving birth to a baby. I don't know whether that is true, but at least I had a slightly better idea regarding what my wife had gone through in giving birth to our children. My pain was further increased by the realization that I was not currently covered under any health insurance policy. My finances were so tight that I couldn't afford *either* the premiums *or* this pending medical bill. Again, I will share a miraculous outcome to this experience in the final chapter.

IT'S TOO QUIET

During the twenty-three years of my first marriage, I occasionally longed for peace and quiet when the kids were around, "cutting up" as only kids can do. After the divorce, I experienced a major overkill in this area. Now there was *way* too much peace and quietness, as I lived all alone with very meager furnishings, in some extremely sub-standard locations.

CHAPTER THREE

I'M SO COLD

I shall never forget living for a time in my brother's old travel trailer. I had borrowed it one summer when I couldn't afford rent to live anywhere else. It had stood unused in his grove for a long time. The furnace didn't work anymore. I parked it at my dad's farm, and needed to utilize his out-door privy, since the bathroom facilities of the trailer could not be used. I shall never forget how cold I got when fall weather hit early, and I couldn't find enough blankets to put over me to keep warm at night. I had grown up on the farm where I slept in an unheated, upstairs bedroom. Thus, I was familiar with sleeping in cold conditions during the winter, but this cold was beyond description. Even today, whenever I get chilled, I vividly recall how cold I got during this period of time.

HOMELESS

Because of my inability to keep rent paid in a timely manner, I encountered several occasions when I really didn't know *where* to live. I feel I can totally identify with those who are completely homeless, and end up living in some very unconventional locations, whether by personal choice or not. Fortunately, my dear Christian friends, Randy and Juli Huber, owners of a local motel, allowed me to spend several weeks living in one of their units, without charge, when I had no other place to go. My extreme living conditions were necessary because I still determined *not* to file bankruptcy, and to pay all of my creditors. Heavy payments were taken out of every commission check to pay debts and child support, leaving me with very little for personal living expenses. I regularly found it necessary to attend Realtor open houses, so I could at least get something to eat once a day when funds were low. I went for nearly two years without a home telephone. This total isolation from the outside world, made the experience of being home alone in the evenings even more difficult to endure. In spite of this major challenge to the success of my business, the Lord continued to bless me, little by little. He gradually led me back to more solid, financial footing, and He provided a more permanent place for me to live. A very kind and understanding landlord allowed me to live in his rental condominium, with full knowledge of my financial situation, and permitted me to pay rent *as* I could, *when* I could. I will be forever grateful to him for his generosity, and I hope to be able to do something, someday, to more adequately make it up to him. This also allowed me to focus more fully on working to clear up the debts which continued to plague me and keep my finances very tight.

YOU'RE UNDER ARREST

One Saturday afternoon, I answered a knock at the door to find a deputy sheriff holding a warrant for my arrest. The charge against me was for a non-sufficient fund check that I had written for less than $20 for gas for my car some time previously. Though my bank usually worked closely with me to prevent this type of thing from being a serious problem, this check had obviously fallen "through the cracks." Now this relatively minor offense had escalated into one of very major proportions. I had to accompany the deputy sheriff to the jail for fingerprinting and mug

---

photos, before being released on my own recognizance, pending a court hearing. This episode didn't contribute anything to improving my sagging feelings of self-esteem. At least the judge was sympathetic enough of my plight to grant a two-year probation, so the matter could be put behind me. Still, it was a very humiliating experience, one that I never want to experience again.

NO MORE JOGGING

One of my favorite morning activities was jogging. I celebrated my fiftieth birthday by running fifty miles during the month of my birthday. About this same time, I noticed that I would start tripping and falling on occasion, when I got tired during the run. After this happened several times, I concluded that maybe I should quit jogging and try something else for exercise and relaxation. In the ensuing months, I found my physical condition continuing to deteriorate. This condition was further aggravated after I was rear-ended in a car accident. I consulted a chiropractor. He eventually referred me to an orthopedic surgeon, who eventually referred me to a neurologist. They did x-rays and put me through several MRIs and other diagnostic tests. They were all puzzled and offered a number of suggestions for treatment, none of which made any significant difference in my condition after I tried them. They were unable to offer me much additional hope for major improvement. In the light of modern medical science and technology, it seemed a most frustrating dilemma. The condition was ultimately diagnosed as spinal myelitis, which produced a condition known as dropped-foot syndrome. In simple terms, this meant it was impossible for me to lift my left leg at will. The messages from my brain to this leg were getting "short-circuited," since the myelin sheathe was damaged. The result was that I had to swing my left leg considerably to clear the ground, so I could walk at all. My walking was more like a waddle, which put additional stress on my spine. Walking was especially challenging in tall grass or plush carpeting. This dilemma is similar to conditions found in people with multiple sclerosis, but my symptoms didn't fit the classic picture of that disease. My left leg felt like a dead weight to my body, though I still had full sensation in it. The medical professionals admitted there was no sure-cure for my condition. Instead, they suggested that the level of stress I had been living with for so long had contributed to my condition. Therefore, the ongoing stress in my life was also a hindrance to my recovery. I will give you a progress report in the final chapter.

NO MORE PLAYING THE ORGAN

This physical condition added another major challenge to my life, since one of my other favorite activities was playing the church organ, something I had done for nearly twenty-five years. Because I couldn't lift my left leg at will, I needed to develop an ingenious way to move that leg on the base pedals. Therefore, I took my left hand from the keyboard whenever the chord changes occurred, and used it to lift and relocate my leg to the proper pedal. My response time was a bit slow at times on certain songs that move more quickly, but most people were totally unaware of the challenge I faced in order to keep playing.

I thank God for the wonderful praise band I played with, as they were always able to help cover up any "goof-ups" that occurred. Ultimately, the church organ was put into storage, and I was allowed to play the piano with the praise band instead of the organ. Thank God I can still at least "tickle the ivories."

If, because of having similar experiences, you are able to identify with *some* of these major challenges that happened in my life over a span of nearly twenty years, you will know that life has certainly been filled with lots of challenge for me. However, it is important to know that, no matter what struggles and pressures we face in life, there is certainly a way to cope, to maintain balance, to keep faith in God, and to experience an optimistic outlook for better days ahead. One storm after another has certainly battered my life, and I have become well-acquainted with grief and pain, but God is still my source, and has given me the ability to hold on until a better day comes. That same power is available to you.

I have to admit that only a handful of people reached out effectively and put their arms around me to help get me back onto "solid ground." So many people just didn't know what to say or do. Nothing seemed to make any sense. Nothing seemed to be simple, normal, life experiences like they knew. Human wisdom was of little value. I found myself pretty much alone, without very many close friends most of the time, except for my precious Lord. He certainly continued to hang in there faithfully, no matter what was going wrong in my life. He was all that I really had left, and I was discovering He was all I really needed.

CHAPTER
4

GOD'S MESSAGE TO ME

Daily prayer and fellowship with the Lord has nearly always been an important part of my Christian life. Thus, it was not something I suddenly decided to initiate now, just because so many things were going wrong in my life at once. I already recognized the desperate importance of getting even more serious about my relationship with the Lord. I had no doubt that God loved me, that He cared about what I was going through, that He had a perfect plan for my life, and that He was fully able to do something dramatic to help me in my devastating circumstances. As I went to the Lord in earnest prayer, I specifically asked Him to show me what He wanted me to do. I know that sometimes God wants us to get up off our seat and go get something worthwhile done. There are other times He just wants us to wait patiently upon Him, and allow Him to do something that only He can do. I wasn't sure what I should do, but I knew that if I would just *trust* Him, He would surely direct me and cause all of these difficulties to develop into something which would please and glorify Him. I knew only that I needed God in my life more than I had ever needed Him before. Only *His* plan, *His* purpose, and *His* power could be counted upon to get me successfully through all of this mess.

By now, I had pretty much forgotten and discarded all the advice I had so faithfully read and studied from the many secular authors, on how to be a great success. I began to focus as never before on what the Word of God had to say to me. As I earnestly sought the face of God, I sensed His Holy Spirit speaking to my heart that there were THREE SPECIFIC THINGS I needed to do in order to survive these major challenges to my faith and life. These three things that He told me to do have since become a lifestyle for me, and I have sincerely attempted to permanently adopt them and use them to govern my life. Though these multiple crisis experiences threatened to destroy my life, my testimony, and my faith in God, I assure you that my obedience to what God's Spirit spoke clearly into my heart has produced a powerful sense of victory, peace, joy, and confidence. They continue to grow and thrive in my life, *in spite of* all that has happened. Regardless, I have come this far by faith, and it is by faith that I shall complete my journey.

After a time, I started feeling that things were quieting down. I was making progress with getting back onto solid ground in most of the problem areas of my life. Then came the phone call in the middle of the night, informing me that my eldest son had been killed in a traffic accident. All kinds of new questions and issues now flooded my heart and mind, as I reeled from this new blow to my life. I don't know how to rank tragedies in their order of trauma and pain, but as devastating as the divorce and the many other tragedies were that occurred in my life, this "every parent's worst nightmare" certainly moved toward the top of that list.

Once more I was driven to my knees to seek the Lord and ask if His advice for me had changed any. I felt that I had been obedient to what He had formerly told me to do, and I wondered if I had simply missed something. However, once again I sensed the Holy Spirit speaking softly that I just needed to *continue* doing the same three things that He had formerly told me to do. At this time, it occurred to me that perhaps I should be sharing this message with other people who are in crisis situations in their lives. Many, many people experience calamities and grasp desperately for all kinds of different solutions to try to deal with their pain. A big percentage of them are not very successful in their search. I don't pretend that this message to me from the Lord contains some form of magic formula or new revelation, because that would be very misleading. What God's message of instruction to me is *really* all about, is a back-to-the-basics approach to building and maintaining a vibrant relationship with the Lord. That relationship must be genuine and alive, so that, no matter what curves life throws at you, you will survive those tragedies or circumstances with the strength and joy that only God can provide.

Though I had been hit with many personal tragedies, I was also fully aware that I was not the only person going through tough times. My situation was really not all that unique. Nevertheless, I have been approached many times by people asking me how I was able to keep going, to maintain such a positive attitude and keep optimistic. Therefore, I felt I must find a way to share the Holy

Spirit's message to me. If it works for me, it will surely work for others too.

Certainly there are still lots of questions that I continue to have as to why everything had to happen to me as it did. I freely acknowledge that I made a lot of major personal mistakes that helped create the mess. Those things were my own fault or stupidity. I have repented to God for them, and I have had to face the fact that I probably *never will* have all of the answers to those questions in this life. God has not chosen to reveal the "whys" of life to me, but I do know that *He knows what He is doing.* He is still in control. He doesn't make mistakes, and He knows just how to get me back on course when I mess up. Furthermore, no matter what is going on, He is still worthy of my praise and worship, whether I feel like giving it to Him or not. He is always worthy, just because *He is God.* Regardless of how we are feeling, or what we are going through, we must not allow anything to have a bearing upon our willingness and desire to *freely praise the Lord.*

The really big question then, for you and me to answer, is this: *Can I really trust God even when He doesn't make perfect sense to me?* I am reminded so often that very seldom does God make perfect sense to at any particular time. I don't have His perspective, His wisdom, or His understanding. Furthermore, I know that I can't even begin to comprehend the depths of His love for me. Therefore, I know that I can respond to that question about trusting God in all things with a resounding "*YES.*" Yes, I can trust God even when He doesn't make sense to me. His track record is perfect. His ways are perfect. His timing is always perfect.

We humans seem to think that we have to figure everything out *right now* or that we have to have specific answers *immediately* to all of our questions in order to put our faith in God. However, it is perfectly okay to admit that we don't know *why*, we don't know *how*, during those times of testing or tragedy in our lives. It is enough to just *let God be God,* to surrender everything in to His hands, and to continue to trust Him, regardless of what we might be able to discern at the moment with our human eyes or minds. The Bible talks often of the importance of "persevering" in our faith. That means to continue trusting God and to keep moving forward by faith, regardless of what is happening, or not happening.

One of the old hymns that expressed my feelings so adequately so many times over the years is the song, THE SOLID ROCK. The Holy Spirit brought the words of this song in particular to me many times, when my grief or pain was so intense that I didn't feel that I could go on any longer.

THE SOLID ROCK
Mote, Edward/Bradbury, William A.
(public domain)

My hope is built on nothing less
Than Jesus' blood and righteousness.
I dare not trust the sweetest frame,
But wholly lean on Jesus' name.

When darkness veils His lovely face,
I rest on His unchanging grace.
In every high and stormy gale,
My anchor holds within the veil.

His oath, His covenant, His blood,
Support me in the whelming flood.
When all around my soul gives way,
He then is all my hope and stay.

When He shall come with trumpet sound,
Oh may I then in Him be found.
Dressed in His righteousness alone,
Faultless to stand before the throne.

Chorus—
On Christ the sold rock I stand,
All other ground is sinking sand.
All other ground is sinking sand.

You might say that I am a real fan of rock music – the kind that is about the *Rock of Ages*. I want to include lyrics from a couple of other special, more recently written songs.

I GO TO THE ROCK OF AGES
Dottie Rambo, copyright 1977
John T. Benson Publishing Company

Where do I go when there's no one else to turn to?
Who do I talk to when no one wants to listen?

Who do I lean on when there's no foundation stable?
I go to the Rock I know that's able, I go to the Rock.

Where do I hide 'til the storms have all passed over?
Where do I run to when the storms of sorrow threaten?
Is there a refuge in the time of tribulation?
When my soul needs consolation, I go to the Rock.

Chorus—
I go to the Rock of my salvation.
Go to the stone that the builder rejected,
Run to the mountain and the mountain stands by me.
When the earth all around me is sinking sand,
Oh Christ the solid Rock I stand.
When I need a shelter, when I need a friend,
I go to the Rock.

I'M ANCHORED IN THE ROCK OF AGES
Gary S. Paxton, Copyright 1978
Christian Grit Music Press

I'm anchored in the Rock of ages,
I'm anchored in the Rock of ages.
No matter how the storm of life thunders and rages,
I'm anchored in the Rock of ages.

Chapter Four

SEEK THE PROVIDER

I can't tell you that I heard an audible voice, as the Spirit of the Lord spoke to me in response to my searching for a way to cope with my "private hell." However, I sensed a very specific, inspirational message which my heart received. This message was further strengthened and enhanced by my knowledge and continued study of God's word, which provided a confirmation absolutely *mandatory* when anyone claims to have "heard a message from the Lord." God will never tell someone to do something that is contrary to instructions already written in the Bible.

The first instruction I felt The Spirit of the Lord speak to me was to:

DRAW CLOSER TO GOD

Now I thought I was already pretty close to God. Many people feel they are pretty close to God, at least *some* of the time. I was already spending considerable time reading my Bible and praying daily. I consistently attended church, and I was intensely involved in generously giving my time to serve many ministries at church and in the community. I was trying to conduct my business and live my life in a way that I *thought* was pleasing to God. However, as I further meditated upon this initial instruction, I realized that I could *indeed* draw a lot closer to the Lord than I was. I then committed my life more completely to the Lord, with a greater focus upon regularly experiencing His wonderful presence in my life. In due season, I determined to set aside at least an hour of my time every day just to pray, read my Bible, and worship the Lord. I entered into a covenant with the Lord to spend more time praying for *other* people and *their* needs, and not to spend so much time praying for myself. I also desired earnestly to allow the Spirit of God to specifically guide my life more effectively on a daily basis, in every decision and dilemma I faced. I didn't determine to do all of this so that I could earn extra "brownie points" with God, to try to prove something to Him, or to demonstrate some level of spiritual achievement in anyone else's eyes. I simply had a sincere desire and interest in building a closer relationship with God. Interestingly, I quickly observed that, the closer I drew to the Lord, the closer I still wanted to draw to Him. The more intimately I knew Him, the more I still wanted to know *Him*, not just things *about* Him. I was reminded of the verse of Scripture in James 4:8, which says: "Draw nigh to God and he will draw nigh to you." Another special verse contains a comment about Jesus made by John the Baptist, in John 3:30, "He must increase and I must decrease." I realized that God had to become my *primary* source of strength and power. He had to become *more important* to me than *anything else* in this entire world. I had to focus upon Jesus, and understand that, no matter what other item I thought I needed at that moment, Jesus was my *full* source and supply. All that I really needed in any situation was simply more of Jesus manifested in and through me. Jesus is referred to in the Hebrew text as Jehovah-Jirah, which means "The Lord provides."

My voice shalt thou hear in the morning,
O LORD, in the morning will I direct my

---

prayer unto thee, and will look up. Psalm 5:3

When thou saidst, Seek ye my face; my heart said unto thee, Thy face, Lord, will I seek. Psalm 27:8

But it is good for me to draw near to God: I have put my trust in the Lord God, that I may declare all thy works. Psalm 73:28

But without faith it is impossible to please him: for he that cometh to God must believe that he is, and that he is a rewarder of them that dilligently seek him. Hebrews 11:6

What does it mean to seek the provider? Throughout the Bible, God uses many names to describe Himself or His attributes as the provider. (The interpretation of the many Hebrew names makes a very fascinating study that I would encourage everyone to investigate). The main point I want to make is that the total fulfillment of every possible need any of us ever faces is found in God, the Source of every good and perfect gift." (James 1:7). That is why I believe the Spirit of God prompted me to focus, first of all, upon drawing closer to Him, closer than I had ever been in my life. He is not only the *Creator God,* He is the God of all provision and strength. He is my attorney, Savior, healer, banner, deliverer, and best friend. He is the shepherd, the Alpha and the Omega, the Lily of the Valley, the Bright and Morning Star, the Fairest of Ten Thousand to my soul, and an endless list of other majestic names, all of which describe a few of His characteristics and attributes. What more could we need than the things which God alone is able to perform and perfect in our lives? God is not transitory, fickle, undependable, or subject to failure, like everything and everyone else on planet earth. Regardless of what challenge or desperate circumstance we might be facing, getting our focus upon the greatness of our God will help us keep everything else in balance.

Jesus is able to provide, one way or the other, anytime of the day or night, anywhere on the earth, above the earth or below the earth, whatever solution, miracle, strength, wisdom, favor, or hope we need. That is why *only* God must get our full attention, not just when we are facing a major crisis or need in our lives, but daily. He must *always* receive all of the glory and the credit for the miraculous answers and supply that occur in our lives. That is why, in spite of the way things may look to us, or to those who are observing us, we don't really need more money, more wisdom, more hope, more friends, more strength, or more of anything else. We just need more of Jesus. He is really *all* that we could *ever* need, both now and throughout eternity.

...looking unto Jesus the author and finisher of our faith... Hebrews 12:2

And ye are complete in Him, which is the head of all principality and power: Colossians 2:10

But seek ye first the Kingdom of God and His righteousness, and all these things shall be added unto you. Matthew 6:33

If we, as born-again Christians *really* believe God's word, we know beyond a shadow of a doubt that God always answers prayer. However, I have observed that God doesn't usually operate on our timetable, or in the way we would usually prefer. We want everything done right now. We don't want to have to go through tough times or pain. That isn't very much fun. We don't want to struggle. We don't want to have to wait for an answer. We are fully acclimated to instant potatoes, instant gravy, microwave chicken, fast car washes, fast food drive-ups, fax machines, high-speed computers, and all of the myriad of other modern conveniences designed to make our lives more productive and efficient. Therefore, we sure don't like to have to spend time waiting *upon* God or *for* God, even if that is exactly what He wants us to do.

When we are faced with the reality and urgency of a need, whether physical, spiritual, emotional, financial, or social, it is very easy for us to totally panic and go ballistic over our situation. We get discouraged and begin to doubt that God's promises in the Bible are really relevant for us today. We wonder whether they really *do* apply to our specific situation. However, this is just another typical lie from Satan. Satan can *never* tell the truth. He lied to Eve in the Garden of Eden, and he has been lying to God's people ever since.

The thief cometh not, but for to steal, and to kill, and to destroy: I am come that they might have life, and that they might have it more abundantly. John 10:10

The work that God is doing in me and through me is a work that is incomplete at this point, but it is a work I find marvelous. I am convinced that the light I see at the "end of the tunnel" is *not* the headlight of a freight train coming my way. It is a work for which only God can receive the praise and glory. I know I could never have made it this far without His grace and assistance. I look forward to experiencing the future chapters, yet to be written in my life, of physical and emotional healing, total deliverance, and complete restoration. In the meantime, the Holy Spirit continues to encourage and strengthen me through two specific things: the *Word of God* and the *music of God.* Through these two ultra-powerful resources, I have personally learned the importance of being *content, rejoicing regardless of my circumstances, and being happy,* as the Apostle Paul describes in Philippians 4:11-13. All of this is possible because *I can indeed do all things through Christ who strengthens me.*

I am amazed at how the words of Scripture or the lyrics of a Gospel song will flow into my heart anytime of the day or night. There are so many nights when I am aware that my inner spirit is singing the lyrics of a Gospel song over and over in my mind. These experiences help me know confidently that, by His Grace, I can make it through *anything*, if I will just keep my eyes upon *Jesus*, not upon my problem.

John 14:26 tells us that the Holy Spirit will bring all things to our remembrance. Therefore, it is very important for us to put, in our minds and hearts, the things that will be valuable for the Holy Spirit to bring to our remembrance during our times of crisis and trial. The responsibility of what we put into our hearts and minds is *ours*, not *His*. The hour of trial will certainly come to us at some point in our lives, and the Holy Spirit will surely be there with us, just as He promised us in Matthew 28:20, "I will never leave you nor forsake you." However, the Word of God and the music of God will be the primary resources that the Holy Spirit will use to help us get through the experience victoriously. Matthew 12:34 declares "out of the abundance of the heart, the mouth speaketh." With God's help, we will find the source of strength and power to rise above each dilemma and struggle. That is because God dwells within us, if we are His children. Therefore, our source, our ability really is there, the place where God dwells. Just to keep the record straight, the only way we can be *one of His children* is to have a personal, intimate relationship with Him by faith through Jesus Christ, His Son. Jesus Himself declared in John chapter three that unless a person is "born again," with a spiritual birthday in addition to a physical birthday, there is no way to enter into the Kingdom of God. Without that most crucial, personal revelation to our hearts, we are stuck in the mire of either dead, dry, deceptive religion or just plain and simple humanism, either of which will create spiritual bankruptcy.

The music of this world, and all of the multitude of books on psychology and positive thinking, will *never* provide us with an "unshakable foundation" that will enable us to cope when "all hell breaks loose around us." Furthermore, we can't do an acceptable job of walking in the Spirit, as believers in God are instructed in the Bible, until we get serious enough about God and His Ways, and begin changing the things we ingest into our hearts and minds.

> *As a man soweth, so shall he also reap.Galatians 6:7*
>
> *Let the words of my mouth, and the meditation of my heart, be acceptable in thy sight, O Lord, my strength, and my redeemer. Psalm 19:14*

Therefore, if we fill our hearts and minds with the ways, the music, and the philosophies of this world, that is the only reservoir the Holy Spirit can draw upon to help us in our time of crisis. He can't bring to our remembrance anything that's not already there. The things of the world certainly won't provide much assistance when we need it so desperately. However, if we fill our minds and hearts with the Word of God and the music of God, those are the lasting treasures that He can bring to our remembrance. He brings the things of true value and substance, the things that provide us with super energy and abundant confidence, so we can rise above and overcome our tragedies. It is really quite simple. If we are not reaping the right things, we have simply not been sowing the right things. That is not God's fault. That is not even the devil's fault. That is *our* fault. We *alone* are in total control of what we watch on television, what we read or listen to, and what we talk about or do in our spare time or recreation, and even what we spend our time dreaming about. We can be sure of this important truth: We *shall* reap what we sow. God's Word is very clear on this cause and effect relationship. Even computer language promises "garbage in, garbage out."

Let not your heart be troubled: Ye believe in God, believe also in me...I am the way, the truth, and the life: no man cometh unto the Father but by me. John 14:1-6

Unless the LORD had been my help, my soul had almost dwelt in silence. When I said, my foot slippeth; thy mercy, O LORD, held me up." Psalm 94:17-18

The righteous shall flourish like the palm tree: he shall grow like a cedar in Lebanon. Those that be planted in the house of the LORD shall flourish in the courts of our God. They shall still bring forth fruit in old age; they shall be fat and flourishing; to show that the LORD is upright: he is my rock, and there is no unrighteousness in him. Psalm 92:12-15

Though I walk in the midst of trouble, thou wilt revive me: thou shalt stretch forth thine hand against the wrath of mine enemies, and thy right hand shall save me. The LORD will perfect that which concerns me." Psalm 138:7-8

And he said unto me, My grace is sufficient for thee: for my strength is made perfect in weakness. Most gladly therefore will I rather glory in my infirmities, that the power of Christ may rest upon me. II Corinthians 12:9

What an awesome God we serve! When we read Scriptures like these, it isn't so difficult for us to begin singing this great Gospel song, one I have loved singing since first hearing it in my childhood:

VICTORY IN JESUS
Eugene M. Bartlett, copyright 1939
Mrs. E.M.Bartlett, Renewed 1967
Assigned Albert E. Brumley and Sons

I heard an old, old story
How a Savior came from glory.
How He gave His life on Calvary
To save a wretch like me.
I heard about His groaning,
Of His precious blood's atoning.
Then I repented of my sin
And won the victory.

I heard about His healing
Of His cleaning pow'r revealing.
How He made the lame to walk again
And caused the blind to see.
And then I cried "dear Jesus,
Come and heal my broken spirit."
And somehow Jesus came and brought
To me the victory.

I heard about a mansion
He has built for me in glory.

> And I heard about the streets of gold
> Beyond the crystal sea.
> About the angels singing
> And the old redemption story.
> And some sweet day I'll sing up there
> The song of victory.
>
> Chorus—
> Oh, Victory in Jesus, my Savior forever.
> He sought me and He bought me with His redeeming blood.
> He loved me 'ere I knew Him and all my love is due Him.
> He plunged me to victory beneath the cleansing blood.

When the storms of life batter us, we don't stand even a slim chance of survival, unless we have something stable to anchor us. We must have something that will be unshaken or unmoved, no matter how vicious or terrifying our experiences. Following are some of the foundational truths of faith we need to understand and utilize for survival, no matter what tragedy or testing comes our way.

JESUS IS OUR BEST INTERCESSOR

No one can deal with our circumstances like Jesus can. He is always working out all of the details of the things happening in our lives, and has only our best interests in mind. He is the best attorney or counselor we could ever hope to have working on our case. He has established a "fiduciary relationship" with us, which means a "law of agency" exists between Jesus and us. This is the same kind of relationship that an attorney has with a client, or a Realtor has with a customer. We're talking about very serious business, because the best interests of the other person are considered before anything else. Because we know that Jesus is perpetually on our side, we can set aside any undue concern about how things will eventually work out. He can always be fully trusted to do the right thing on our behalf. What a great relief that should be to us!

> *Wherefore he is able also to save them to the uttermost that come unto God by him, seeing he ever liveth to make intercession for them. For such an high priest became us, who is holy, harmless, undefiled, separate from sinners, and made higher than the heavens; Hebrews 7:25*
>
> *For we have not an high priest which cannot be touched with the feeling of our infirmities; but was in all points tempted like we are, yet without sin. Let us therefore come boldly unto the throne of grace, that we may obtain mercy, and find grace to help in time of need. Hebrews 4:15-16*

THERE'S SOMETHING ABOUT THAT NAME
Bill and Gloria Gaither, copyright 1970 William J. Gaither

Jesus, Jesus, Jesus,
There's just something about that name.
Master, Savior, Jesus,
Like the fragrance after the rain;
Jesus, Jesus, Jesus,
Let all Heaven and earth proclaim;
Kings and Kingdoms will all pass away,
But there's something about that name.

JESUS IS OUR COMPLETE HAPPINESS

When the world thinks of joy and happiness, it thinks of happiness as something to be acquired, achieved, grasped or discovered. The primary focus is, "If only I could have…, I'd be happy. If only I could be…, I'd be happy. If only I could do…, I'd be happy." The blanks could be filled in with an endless array of ideas, limited only by one's imagination. We all know many people who have this faulty concept of happiness. No wonder it becomes so elusive, so unachieved and so difficult to understand. Happiness is really *better* defined as a state of mind, a present substance, a method of travel, a basic attitude of life. You either have it or you don't. There's no in-between. It is intrinsic, not extrinsic. Sometimes, the more that happiness is pursued as a goal, the more elusive it becomes. It is only truly present when we have Jesus within our hearts, as the Lord of our hearts. That is when we know what real happiness is all about. True happiness is experienced within our hearts. It is not out somewhere beyond us, playing hide and seek with us.

> *The joy of the LORD is your strength. Nehemiah 8:10*
>
> *These things have I spoken unto you, that my joy might remain in you, and that your joy might be full. John 15:11*
>
> *...when his glory shall be revealed, ye may be glad also with exceeding joy.   I Peter 4:13*
>
> *Rejoice evermore. Pray without ceasing. In every thing give thanks: for this is the will of God in Christ Jesus concerning you. 1 Thessalonians 5:16-18*

Another very precious gospel song that I love to sing and play is this one. It sums up my complete personal testimony in just a few verses.

THE LONGER I SERVE HIM
William J. Gaither, Gloria Gaither
copyright 1965, William J. Gaither, Inc.

Since I started for the Kingdom,
Since my life He controls,
Since I gave my heart to Jesus,
The longer I serve Him, the sweeter He grows.

Ev'ry need He is supplying,
Plenteous grace He bestows.
Ev'ry day my way gets brighter;
The longer I serve Him, the sweeter He
grows.

Chorus—
The longer I serve Him the sweeter He
grows;
The more that I love Him, more love He
bestows.
Each day is like heaven, my heart
overflows;
The longer I serve Him the sweeter He
grows.

JESUS IS OUR COMPLETE ABILITY TO COPE

There *will* be better days ahead. You and I *must* believe that. Jesus alone can provide us with the needed confidence and assurance that we shall overcome and prevail. Regardless of what others have done *to us*, or what we might have done *to ourselves*, Jesus alone will provide the ability to persevere. We can keep moving forward in the face of massive pressure from our circumstances. We can make it. Yes, we can! I especially love the lyrics to this song written by Mike Murdock, a man whose ministry has had a profound, positive impact on my life.

> **I CAN MAKE IT**
> *Mike Murdock*
>
> I can make it. I can make it.
> This trial I'm going through,
> God's going to show me just what to do.
> I can make it. I can make it.
> I don't care what's going wrong.
> God won't let it last too long,
> 'Cause I'm not in this thing alone.
> I can make it.

Can you imagine the impact on your life if you jumped out of bed every morning and began singing that song? Coping with the pressures of life really depends a great deal upon what you focus your attention upon. If you focus only upon the problem or dilemma, you will automatically find that it growing larger in your vision. However, if you focus upon Jesus and the multitude of special promises contained in His Word, you will find Him becoming much bigger than the problem or dilemma.

> *Why art thou cast down, O my soul? And why art thou disquieted within me? Hope thou in God; for I shall yet praise him, who is the health of my countenance, and my God. Psalm 42:11*
>
> *...David encouraged himself in the LORD his God. 1 Samuel 30:6*

If you read the entire passage of Scripture prior to this verse, you get a better understanding of the fact that nothing was going very well for David at this point in his life. He wasn't able to get much encouragement from either his friends or his army, because they were all also at their wit's end. Life was tough, and it didn't appear things were going to be getting better anytime soon. Nevertheless, David took control over his fears and his worry, realizing that the Lord was a whole lot bigger than his present problem. David survived this episode victoriously by getting his focus shifted from his problem to his provider. This was a very important step that David needed to take for himself. He couldn't wait for someone else to do it for him. That's also what we need to do. However, in order for someone to encourage himself in the Lord, he needs to *know* the Lord. The only way to really *know* the Lord, is to spend quality time with Him. The best way to spend time with Him is in prayer and reading of His Word, the Bible. Time spent this way will allow powerful communication to flow both ways, and the more you know *about* the Lord, the better you will know *Him*. The better you know Him, the more you will understand of His wonderful ability to help you in every situation.

The righteous cry, and the Lord heareth, and delivereth them out of all their troubles. Many are the afflictions of the righteous; but the Lord delivereth him out of them all. Psalm 34:17, 19

And this is the confidence that we have in him, that, if we ask anything according to his will, he heareth us: And if we know that he hear us, whatsoever we ask, we know that we have the petitions that we desired of him. 1 John 5:14-15

"But ye, Beloved, building up yourselves on your most holy faith, praying in the Holy Ghost." Jude 20

JESUS IS OUR BEST HEALER

Jesus is the Great Physician. The Hebrew word to describe Him in that capacity is Jehovah-rapha, "the Lord who heals you." There are many, many people alive on earth today who are just like the woman Jesus encountered in the crowd one day. The Bible describes her as a person who had spent all she had on doctors, but her condition was no better. Does this describe the condition of anyone you know? It's easy to spend endless sums on doctors, considering the cost of modern medical treatments. Regardless of the ailment or symptoms, there is much confusing medical advice. Supposed "sure-cures" are often promoted by both professionals and non-professionals, as long as the money, health insurance plan or Medicare holds out. We tend to run here and there, looking for medical solutions, many times becoming more frustrated and broke in the process. I am not saying we shouldn't consult with the best available medical advice available. However, many doctors will usually eventually admit, that unless God does the healing, no cure will occur. New illnesses and diseases seem to appear faster than cures can be found, and there is a growing list of diseases for which there is no known cure. Therefore, if God has to do the healing anyway, why not begin by looking to Him for the solution a lot sooner? He still might direct you to a good doctor. You still might need surgery or a prescribed medical treatment, but the ultimate healer is still the Lord God, Jehovah-rapha.

Furthermore, it matters not whether the needed healing is physical, emotional, mental, or financial. Jesus is *still* always the best solution. He *alone* can mend a broken heart and deal with the emotional scars or painful memories. He *alone* can get you out of that mess and back onto solid ground. He can deal not only with the *result* of the mess, but also with the *root cause.*

> *Is any sick among you? let him call for the elders of the church; and let them pray over him, anointing him with oil in the name of the Lord: And the prayer of faith shall save the sick, and the Lord shall raise him up; and if he have committed sins, they shall be forgiven him. James 5:14-15*
>
> *Surely he hath borne our griefs, and carried our sorrows: yet we did esteem him stricken, smitten of God, and afflicted. But he was wounded for our transgressions, he was bruised for our iniquities: the chastisement of our peace was upon him; and with his stripes we are healed. Isaiah 53:4-5*
>
> *Bless the Lord, O my soul, and forget not all his benefits; who forgiveth all thine iniquities, who healeth all thy diseases. Psalm 103:2-3*

To accompany those Scriptures on healing, this prayer chorus we occasionally sing fits right in:

> **I AM THE LORD**
> *Don Moen, copyright 1986*
> *Integrity's Hosanna! Music*
>
> I am the God that healeth thee.
> I am the Lord, your healer;
> I sent My Word and healed your disease,
> I am the Lord, your healer.

JESUS IS OUR PEACE

One of the things the angels announced at Jesus' birth was news concerning *peace on earth*. What peace were they talking about? Where is it? How can it be found? It certainly doesn't appear to be a very available commodity on earth today. We are not surrounded by peace, but rather by the things that destroy peace. I recently heard that there are presently forty different wars or areas of conflict in progress in the world. The only genuine peace that is available to us *at all* is an inner peace. That peace can come to us only through Jesus Christ. He is called Jehovah-shalom, "the God of peace."

I am not talking about denying the real facts of life and trying to live in an artificial vacuum of some kind, where we lose touch with reality. The peace that is available to us through Jesus Christ is a peace that definitely is *not* of this world. It is a peace that the world can't give, and the world can't take away.

I remember a story about a contest held several years ago. Many artists were challenged to come up with a painting best depicting, through their art, the subject of peace. Some of them took up the challenge and prepared their very best scenes to be entered in the competition. There were paintings containing pastoral scenes of quietness and contentment, depicting animals or nature at rest. However, the painting that won the first-place ribbon depicted a very different scene, a rocky shoreline along the ocean. A storm was pounding the coast with massive waves. Ominous clouds and jagged lightning filled the sky. To the casual observer, there was nothing peaceful about this painting, except for the mother bird perched high in a cleft of the rock. She was sitting peacefully on her nest, protecting her eggs. She, in turn, was protected from the storm, because she was hidden in safety high above the angry water, in a crevice of the solid rock cliff. She was in total peace and security, though she was surrounded by a raging storm. There was nothing for her to worry about. The rock was solid and she was safe, as long as she stayed put. I identify with that mother bird in many ways, because of the various stormy situations I have encountered in life. In spite of those storms, I can testify of experiencing God's perfect peace, because I knew the Rock of Ages would remain my adequate protection, and I knew I would survive the vicious storm intact.

> *Peace I leave with you, my peace I give unto you: not as the world giveth, give I unto you. Let not your heart be troubled, neither let it be afraid. John 14:27*

Thou wilt keep him in perfect peace, whose mind is stayed on thee: because he trusteth in thee. Isaiah 26:3

These things I have spoken unto you, that in me ye might have peace. In the world ye shall have tribulation, but be of good cheer; I have overcome the world. John 16:33

And the peace of God, which passeth all understanding, shall keep your hearts and minds through Christ Jesus. Philippians 4:7

Now the Lord of peace give you peace always by all means. II Thessalonians 3:16

God is our refuge and strength, a very present help in trouble. Therefore will not we fear, though the earth be removed, and though the mountains be carried into the midst of the sea: Psalm 46:1-2

There are many more Scriptures on peace than the ones I have listed. There are also some very special songs I'd like to include about the peace of God.

For his anger endureth but a moment; in his favor is life: weeping may endure for a night, but joy cometh in the morning. Psalm 30:5

JOY COMES IN THE MORNING
William J. Gaither, Gloria Gaither
copyright 1974, William J. Gaither, Inc.

If you've knelt beside the rubble of an
aching, broken heart.
When the things you gave your life to fell
apart,
You're not the first to be acquainted with
sorrow, grief or pain,
But the Master promised sunshine after rain.

To invest your seed of trust in God, in
mountains you can't move.
You have risked your life on things you
cannot prove.
But to give the things you cannot keep, for
what you cannot lose,
Is the way to find the joy God has for you.

Chorus—
Hold on my child, joy comes in the morning,
Weeping only lasts for the night.
Hold on my child, joy comes in the morning,
The darkest hour means dawn is just in
sight.

WONDERFUL PEACE

Warren Cornell/George W. Cooper
(public domain)

Far away in the depths of my spirit tonight
Rolls a melody sweeter than psalm;
In celestial-like strains it unceasingly flows
O'er my soul like an infinite calm.

What a treasure I have in the wonderful
peace,
Buried deep in the heart of my soul,
So secure that no power can mine it away
While the years of eternity roll.

And me-thinks when I rise to that city of
peace,
Where the Author of peace I shall see,
That one strain of the song which the
ransomed will sing
In that heavenly kingdom shall be.

Ah, soul, are you here without comfort or
rest,
Marching down the rough pathway of time?
Make Jesus your friend 'ere the shadows
grow dark.
O accept this sweet peace so sublime.

Chorus—
Peace, peace, wonderful peace,
Coming down from the Father above.
Sweep over my spirit forever, I pray,
In fathomless billows of love.

JESUS IS ALWAYS WORTHY OF WORSHIP

It doesn't matter what is happening or not happening. It doesn't matter how we feel. It doesn't matter how impossible things look at the present. It doesn't matter who did what to whom. Instead of being overwhelmed by our circumstances, we need to keep our attention focused upon Jesus. We need to continue worshipping and praising Him, no matter what we are experiencing. The Bible tells us that God dwells in our praise. That is His "mailing address," and that is where we will always find Him. If we praise the Lord, even when we don't understand why things are happening as they are, this activity of faith will help us keep our perspective and balance. This applies especially when we don't *feel* like praising Him. From a human perspective, it might not even make *any sense* to praise Him. However, praising the Lord will ultimately bring about the needed victory in our lives. When we praise the Lord, we are expressing our *total dependency* upon Him, and our devotion and love to Him. Thus, we literally drive out, or replace, the feelings of worry, despair, and hopelessness. Many powerful moves of God have occurred as God's people began praising and worshipping Him, instead of griping, complaining or feeling fearful of the uncertainties of the future.

The sixteenth chapter of Acts tells a fascinating story about Paul and Silas, who were missionaries in the early church. They had been arrested, beaten, and locked in stocks in the inner dungeon of the local prison, simply because they had been used of God to bring healing and deliverance to a demon-possessed girl. This was no decent way for a couple of God's special ambassadors to be treated, simply because they wanted to help someone with a desperate need. They could easily have wondered if God really knew what was going on that night. However, the Scriptures tell us that, around midnight, Paul and Silas were praying and singing hymns unto the Lord. In spite of the pain from their wounds and the embarrassment of being arrested, in spite of the unfairness of their treatment, and in spite of this unexpected turn of events in their ministry, they refused to whine and complain. The other prisoners, incarcerated there that night, took special note of this most unusual response from these men of God, and they listened as the sound of singing filtered through the prison. Perhaps they wondered whether there *really was* something to the message of salvation that Paul and Silas had been preaching. As Paul and Silas continued their songs of praise and worship to the Lord, suddenly an earthquake struck the prison. This was a genuine "jail-house rock." Not only were Paul and Silas' feet and hands released from the stocks, and the prison doors miraculously blown open, but also all of the other prisoners were immediately and supernaturally released. As a result of this miracle, the jailer and his entire family accepted God's plan of salvation for themselves. What a happy conclusion, simply because two preachers of the Gospel chose to worship and praise the Lord, though it would have been a lot easier to simply wallow in their pain and misery, thinking God must have forgotten about them and abandoned them.

I would like to highlight a couple of thoughts regarding this incident. One of these thoughts is the importance of praising the Lord even when it is difficult to do. This is a major key that brought about the deliverance of Paul and Silas from their jail cell. They chose the *best* thing to do in their pain, not the easy or expected thing. The Lord met them at the point of their desperate need, and delivered them instantaneously. They soon forgot about the injustice of their situation, because they began seeing the Lord as being much bigger than their circumstances. God was worthy of their praise, no matter how they felt. They had no idea, ahead of time, that God was going to use their miserable predicament to meet them in a special way, to minister His grace and power *to* them and *through* them.

The other thought I would like to highlight is that, not only were Paul and Silas set free from their prison cell, but every *other* prisoner in that prison was also set free that evening. Even the jailer and his entire family were set free from the bondage of their sin. When things go wrong in our lives, and we see our situation as being totally hopeless and out of control, that is the perfect opportunity for God to bring about the kind of results that only *He* can achieve, in spite of our pain. We just need to worship and praise Him, regardless. No matter what may happen to us in this life, the end result, the bottom-line outcome must be that there will be a positive impact upon the lives of others around us. They must be able to observe, first hand, the power of God actually working in our lives. A miracle that God could easily perform to bring about a solution to a need in *our* lives, would not be completely worthwhile, unless there was also a positive impact on the lives of *others*. Others must be faced with the necessity of knowing the same God you and I serve. What better way for that to happen, than for them to observe God working powerfully in and through us? God is always interested in people, and He will do whatever it takes to bring them to an understanding of His eternal plan of salvation. That is why Jesus came to earth in the first place.

Once they learned the eventual outcome of their prison experience, I wonder how Paul and Silas would respond if they were asked whether their experience had been worthwhile. They refused to have a pity party, though one could certainly have been justified, according to the human, natural way of thinking. Their decisive action allowed God to move on their behalf in a most glorious way. They focused upon their source of power. As a result, many lives were dramatically changed forever. Just imagine how differently the story would have turned out if Paul and Silas had chosen to act like most of us would under the same circumstances.

> *Although the fig tree shall not blossom, neither shall fruit be in the vines; the labour of the olive shall fail, and the fields shall yield no meat; the flock shall be cut off from the fold, and there shall be no herd in the stalls. Yet I will rejoice in the LORD, I will joy in the God of my salvation. Habakkuk 3:17-18*

The key thought of this Scripture is that, no matter what happens, I *will* praise the Lord. I make a conscious decision to praise the Lord, *in spite of* my circumstances. God is worthy of my praise, regardless of what is happening, or not happening in my life.

I will bless the LORD at all times: His praise shall continually be in my mouth.
Psalms 34:1

I also love these great praise songs:

PRAISE THE LORD
Brown Bannister and Mike Hudson
copyright 1978, Word Music, Inc.

When you're up against a struggle that shatters all your dreams,
And your hopes have been crushed by Satan's manifested schemes,
And you feel the urge within you to submit to earthly fears,
Don't let the faith you're standin' in seem to disappear
Now Satan is a liar and he tries to make us think that we are paupers
When he knows himself we're children of the King.
So lift up the mighty shield of faith, the battle has been won.
We know that Jesus Christ is risen, and the work's already done.

Chorus—
Praise the Lord, He can work through those who praise Him.
Praise the Lord, for our God inhabits praise.
Praise the Lord, for the chains that seem to

bind you,
Serve only to remind you, That they drop
powerless behind you
When you praise Him.

LET'S JUST PRAISE THE LORD
William J. and Gloria Gaither
copyright 1972, William J. Gaither, Inc.

O, We thank You for Your kindness;
We thank You for Your love.
We've been in heavenly places;
Felt blessings from above.
We've been sharing all the good things
The family can afford.
Let's just turn our praise toward heaven
And praise the Lord.
Just the precious name of Jesus
Is worthy of our praise.
Let us bow our knee before Him;
Our hand toward heaven raise.
When He come in clouds of glory
With Him to ever reign,
Let's lift our happy voices
And praise His dear Name.

Chorus—
Let's just praise the Lord. Praise the Lord.
Let's just lift our hearts to heaven and praise
the Lord.
Let's just praise the Lord. Praise the Lord.
Let's just lift our hearts to heaven and praise
the Lord.

JESUS IS ABSOLUTELY OUR BEST FRIEND

Jesus' love for us is unconditional. He loves us not because of *what* we do, but because of *who* we are and *whose* we are. We belong to Him. He died for us. No matter what happens, He will always be there for us. He promised to never leave us nor forsake us. He will always remain faithful. He will provide a way *through*, a way *around*, a way *under*, or a way *over* whatever mountain or difficulty may be facing us. He will complete that which He has started in us. Nobody, absolutely nobody loves us like He does. The interesting thing is that He knows everything there is to know about us, the good as well as the bad. Yet, He *still* loves us.

> NO, NOT ONE!
> *Rev. Johnson Oatman, Jr.*
> *George C. Hugg, (public domain)*
>
> There's not a friend like the lowly Jesus,
> No, not one! No, not one!
> None else could heal all our souls' diseases,
> No, not one! No, not one!
>
> No friend like Him is so high and holy,
> No, not one! No, not one!
> And yet no friend is so meek and lowly,
> No, not one! No, not one!
>
> There's not an hour that He is not near us,
> No, not one! No, not one!
> No night so dark but His love can cheer us,
> No, not one! No, not one!

Did ever saint find this Friend forsake him?
No, not one! No, not one!
Or sinner find that He would not take him?
No, not one! No, not one!

Was e'er a gift like the Savior given?
No, not one! No, not one!
Will He refuse us a home in heaven?
No, not one! No, not one!

Chorus—
Jesus knows all about our struggles.
He will guide till the day is done.
There's not a friend like the lowly Jesus,
No, not one! No, not one!

and there is a friend that sticketh closer than a brother. Proverbs 18:24

But the Lord is faithful, who shall stablish you, and keep you from evil. 2 Thessalonians 3:3

There hath no temptation taken you but such as is common to man: but God is faithful, who will not suffer you to be tempted above that ye are able; but will with the temptation also make a way to escape, that ye may be able to bear it. I Corinthians 10:13

This beloved old hymn is so appropriate to share with you right here.

WHAT A FRIEND
*Joseph M. Scriven/Charles C.
Converse, (public domain)*

What a friend we have in Jesus,
All our sins and griefs to bear.
What a privilege to carry
Everything to God in prayer.
Oh, what peace we often forfeit,
Oh, what needless pain we bear.
All because we do not carry
Everything to God in prayer.

Have we trials and temptations?
Is there trouble anywhere?
We should never be discouraged;
Take it to the Lord in prayer.
Can we find a friend so faithful,
Who will all our sorrows share?
Jesus knows our every weakness;
Take it to the Lord in prayer.

Are we weak and heavy-laden,
Cumbered with a load of care?
Precious Savior, still our refuge.
Take it to the Lord in prayer.
Do thy friends despise forsake thee?
Take it to the Lord in prayer.
In His arms He'll take and shield thee;
Thou wilt find a solace there.

STAY IN PROPER ATTITUDE

The second of the three steps spoken by the Spirit of the Lord to my heart, for my survival and recovery when experiencing the storms of life was:

COUNT YOUR BLESSINGS.
QUIT FEELING SORRY FOR YOURSELF.

It is so normal to focus only on our problems when troubles and difficulties come our way. We hold our problems close to our hearts, and spend countless hours thinking about all of the possessions, the position, or the people we have lost. As a result, we end up experiencing a *major pity-party* that becomes so massive we just can't seem to bring it to a close. We can easily justify our actions, and sincerely believe we deserve this pity-party, in light of all that has happened to us. That is very normal and human. However, from my own experience, I strongly felt the Lord telling me to focus, instead, on all the things I *still* possessed, not the things I had lost. I needed to focus upon everything I could still be thankful for. I needed to realize anew, that there were people all over the world going through tough times just as tragic as mine. My dilemma was not really all that unique. I needed to take control of my thoughts and quit thinking negative, self-condemning thoughts. I needed to start thinking more about how big *God* is, and about how much He loves me. I needed to remind myself about God's many, many promises to bring me into complete victory and blessing as *more than a conqueror*, all in His time.

COUNT YOUR BLESSINGS
Rev. Johnson Oatman Jr./ Edwin O. Excell, (public domain)

When upon life's billows you are tempest-tossed,
When you are discouraged, thinking all is lost.
Count your many blessings, name them one by one,
And it will surprise you what the Lord hath done.

Are you ever burdened with a load of care?
Does the cross seem heavy you are called to bear?
Count your many blessings, every doubt will fly,
And you will be singing as the days go by.

When you look at others with their lands and gold,
Think that Christ has promised you His wealth untold.
Count your many blessings money cannot buy
Your reward in Heaven nor your home on high.

So, amid the conflict, whether great or small,
Do not be discouraged, God is over all.
Count your many blessings angels will

attend,
Help and comfort give you to your journey's end.
Chorus—
Count your blessings name them one by one;
Count your blessings see what God hath done;
Count your blessings name them one by one;
Count your many blessings see what God hath done.

Sitting around feeling sorry for ourselves serves only to extend the period of defeat, bondage, discouragement, and despair we are experiencing. In that state of mind, we really are just having ego and pride problems, only we are stuck in reverse instead of in drive, thus working a powerful, negative impact in our lives. Our focus is still upon ourselves, upon what *we* need, upon what *we* don't have, or upon *our* pain and grief. There are many people who choose to simply camp beside their pain and suffering, and then remain there for the rest of their lives. Their lack of faith and trust in God to deliver them prevents Him from effectively bringing them *through* their unpleasant circumstances to victory on the other side. We have the ability to completely hamstring God from demonstrating His power and ability to come mightily to our assistance. Our continued focus upon how *tough* things are has the negative effect of drawing attention only to us, instead of focusing on how big and powerful *God* is. You probably know people like this. They are completely hung up on the thought, "Oh, poor

---

me. I've got it so tough. Nobody knows the trouble I've seen." Sometimes people even appear to take great pleasure in the fact that *their* pain and grief is far *worse* than anyone else's. What a mess to be in! If we continue to think we are the only ones who are facing tough times, we end up making ourselves sicker, not better. No matter how tough things get for us, we must focus upon the things that we *still* have, not on the things we have lost. Every day of our lives should be "Thanksgiving Day," when we remember all of our blessings.

II Chronicles chapter 20:12 in the Old Testament tells the story of a king named Jehosophat, who unexpectedly found himself facing a major crisis. His country, Israel, was completely surrounded by an enemy's army. He received a letter from them, demanding their immediate and absolute surrender. The king called the leaders and the people of the nation to immediate prayer and fasting before the Lord for His help during this crisis. I especially love this portion of his prayer; "Neither do we know what to do: but our eyes are upon thee." There are many times in my life when I feel the same way when I pray. *Nothing* seems to make any sense. There seems to be *no way* through a crisis. Life isn't fair. However, when I don't know what else to do, the only thing that I can sensibly do is keep my eyes upon the Lord, and not panic over my circumstances.

All of us should take time to read the rest of Jehosophat's story. Only then will we fully appreciate the unbelievable miracle the Lord performed for the Israelites that day, though the odds for victory were definitely stacked against them. Their key to victory was obedience to the

Lord, and recognition that the battle was *His*, not theirs. Thus, they approached the battle in a most unusual manner. The king had the church choir members lead the army to the battlefield. As they walked along toward the battlefield, they sang songs of worship and praise unto the Lord. Their "secret weapon" was their focus upon the Source of their deliverance, rather than upon their ability to defend themselves. Upon arrival at the battlefield, they discovered their enemy had already been defeated by a miracle from the Lord. They didn't have to fire a single shot. The Lord didn't fail them. He delivered them even *before* they got to the battlefield. Instead of running from the enemy, they spent a long time looting the items left lying around.

The Lord also will be a refuge for the oppressed, a refuge in times of trouble. And they that know thy name will put their trust in thee; for thou, Lord, hast not forsaken them that seek thee. Psalm 9:9-10

Some trust in chariots, and some in horses; but we will remember the name of the Lord our God. Psalm 20:7

Take, my brethren, the prophets, who have spoken in the name of the Lord, for an example of suffering affliction, and of patience. Behold, we count them happy which endure. Ye have heard of the patience of Job, and have seen the end of the Lord; that the Lord is very pitiful, and of tender mercy. James 5:10-11

The Bible is full of stories of people who endured unfair treatment and difficulties. However, they stayed true to their faith. They obeyed God, no matter what He asked them to do, and they never regretted the outcome. God always came to their rescue, one way or the other. See Hebrews 11 for a long list of God's "Hall of Faith" candidates.

Of course, we can't stand on the promises of God, if we don't know what they are. Just knowing John 3:16 or the twenty-third Psalm, is unlikely to make a major difference in our ability to calmly face the evil forces of Satan, when he attacks. The Word of God is one of our most valuable weapons for defeating our enemy. Therefore, we dare not take an apathetic approach to our study and knowledge of the Word of God.

> *For though we walk in the flesh, we do not war after the flesh: For the weapons of our warfare are not carnal, but mighty through God to the pulling down of strongholds, 2 Corinthians 10:3-4*
>
> *O how love I thy law! It is my meditation all the day. Thy word is a lamp unto my feet, and a light unto my path. Psalm 119:96,97,105*
>
> *...some trust in chariots, and some in horses: but we will remember the name of the Lord, our God. Psalm 20:7*

The words to this praise chorus help sum up my thoughts at this point:

MIGHTILY IN ME
David Ingles
copyright 1978, David Ingles Music

The Word is working mightily in me.
The Word is working mightily in me.
No matter what my circumstance,
Or what I feel or see,
For the Word is working mightily in me.

STAY ON THE PREMISES

The third and final step I felt the Spirit of the Lord impress upon my heart as a necessary step to my healing and restoration during the tough times of life, was that I should:

STAY BUSY AND PRODUCTIVE

I felt that this message applied specifically to my continued involvement in the affairs of the Kingdom of God. The usual thing that happens to so many people when they face tough times, intense grief and pain, or just the everyday struggles of life, is that they choose to drop out. They drop out of church. They drop out of relationships with dear friends. They drop out of anything that stirs up feelings or memories of another time or another place. Instead of continuing to rub shoulders with people who know and love them, they choose to become a recluse, a hermit, or an absentee. They start drifting from their moorings and get blown "out to sea" aimlessly, because they don't remain steadfast in what they know is right. They even drift from church to church, not staying too long in any one place, because they don't want anyone to find out too much about them.

There is an adage, "Idle hands are the devil's workshop." Perhaps your parents shared that with you when you were growing up. It is very true that anytime someone has too much time on their hands, there is *far* too much opportunity to stew on problems, to commiserate on all of the things that happened or were said. This only leads to more misery, because everything appears to get worse, not better. Getting God's children sidetracked in this manner is a favorite trick of Satan. Thus God's people become ineffective and unproductive in His kingdom. Satan loves to get individuals and even entire churches involved in simply being spectators, rather than participators in what God is doing. At this point, it is easy to become critical of others, and get involved in gossip or other similar counter-productive activities, which only bring the advancement of the Kingdom of God to a screeching halt.

When problems and difficulties come into our lives, this is the perfect time to get *really* serious about the strength and love that is available to us though the spiritual ministry of the Body of Christ, the Church. This is certainly *not* the time to go AWOL (absent without official leave) and disappear from needed fellowship. This is not the time to go into hiding, to withdraw, to try to go it alone. We desperately need each other, especially when we are hurting so badly. This is the very reason God called us to become part of His Body. We need Him and we need each other. All parts of the Body of Christ are divinely designed to minister to the needs of the other parts. This is true physically and spiritually. Even as others are to minister to us in our time of need, we are to minister to them in theirs. Thus, not only are *we* robbed of their help when we withdraw, but also the rest of the Body of Christ is robbed of our ministry to them. Then only Satan's plan is achieved. We must never become like a rock skipping across a pond, with no one knowing for sure where we will finally land. We must *keep on* keeping on. There is great merit in steadfast, persevering people. *Don't ever give up!* The Bible teaches that we will continue to reap exactly as we have sown, as long as we remain faithful.

> *But this I say: He who soweth sparingly shall reap also sparingly, and he who soweth bountifully shall reap also bountifully. As every man purposeth in his heart, so let him give, not grudgingly or out of compulsion; for God loveth the cheerful giver. And God is able to make all grace abound toward you, that ye, always having a sufficiency in all things, may abound in every good work. As it is written: "He hath dispersed abroad, he hath given to the poor; his righteousness remaineth for ever." 2 Corinthians 9:6-9*

The Rock of our Salvation still stands unmoved as an anchor for us to remain firmly attached to. He will endure and remain faithful to us. We can trust Him implicitly. He will never fail us. Therefore, there is no need for God's children to start drifting, to become wishy-washy, and to be blown about by the tough circumstances of life. Our hope is secure and enduring. Therefore, in order for the power of God to be manifested in our lives during those tough times of life, these are some of the things that we need to do to make sure that we are doing in our lives.

STAY FAITHFUL TO CHURCH

Bear ye one another's burdens, and so fulfill the law of Christ. Galatians 6:2

not forsaking the assembling of ourselves together, as is the manner of some, but exhorting one another, and so much the more as ye see the Day approaching. Hebrews 10:25

STAY FAITHFUL IN PRAYER

I say unto you, though he will not rise and give to him because he is his friend, yet because of his importunity he will rise and give him as many as he needeth. And I say unto you: ask, and it shall be given you; seek, and ye shall find; knock, and it shall be opened unto you. For every one that asketh receiveth, and he that seeketh findeth, and to him that knocketh it shall be opened. Luke 11:8-10

Again I say unto you, that if two of you shall agree on earth as touching anything that they shall ask, it shall be done of my

108 *HOW TO KEEP YOUR FAITH*

Father which is in heaven. Matthew 18:19

Therefore let them that suffer according to the will of God commit the keeping of their souls to Him in well doing, as unto a faithful Creator. 1 Peter 4:19

And let us not be weary in well doing; for in due season we shall reap if we faint not. Galatians 6:9

These verses emphasize the importance of continuing to do the right thing indefinitely, even when going through a tough time. Otherwise, we will never see the fruit from the good things we have sown. We can't quit doing the right thing, just because our circumstances don't change immediately.

But we have this treasure in earthen vessels, that the excellency of the power may be of God, and not of us. We are troubled on every side, yet not distressed; we are perplexed, but not in despair; persecuted, but not forsaken; cast down, but not destroyed; 2 Corinthians 4:7-9

It would seem that the apostle Paul knows something very important about surviving tough times. Regardless of what happens, we can never afford to just sit down and quit. Even if we are knocked down, we must get up again and keep going, so that the power of God, the treasure within us, can be properly displayed to the world around us.

This song contains some powerful thoughts for our consideration:

WE'VE COME THIS FAR BY FAITH
Albert A Goodson, copyright 1963
Manna Music, Inc.

Don't be discouraged with trouble in your life;
He'll bear your burdens, and move all discord and strife.
Just remember the good things He has done;
Things that seemed impossible,
Oh, praise Him for the vict'ries He has won.

Chorus—
Oh, we've come this far by faith, leaning on the Lord;
Trusting in His holy Word, He's never failed us yet.
Oh, We can't turn back, We've come this far by faith.

STAY FAITHFUL TO THE LORD

A plant is filled with life and productivity as it puts its roots down into the soil in which it is planted. So it is with us. We will be fruitful and productive as we draw our strength from the Lord.

> *As ye have therefore received Christ Jesus the LORD, so walk ye in him; rooted and built up in him and stablished in the faith, as ye have been taught, abounding therein with thanksgiving. Colossians 2:6-7*
>
> *I am the vine, ye are the branches. He that abideth in me, and I in him, the same bringeth forth much fruit: for without me ye can do nothing. John 15:5*

STAY FAITHFUL IN LIFESTYLE

We need to demonstrate to the world and to other believers how a Christian copes with pressures and perseveres in the trials of life. No matter what is happening, believers are never to go around looking like they are an "accident going somewhere to happen." Never forget that we are winners, not losers.

> *Be not deceived, God is not mocked; for whatsoever a man soweth, that shall he also reap. For he that soweth to his flesh shall of the flesh reap corruption; but he that soweth to the Spirit shall of the Spirit reap life everlasting. And let us not be weary in welldoing, for in due season we shall reap, if we faint not. As we therefore*

HOW TO KEEP YOUR FAITH **111**

> *have opportunity, let us do good unto all*
> *men, especially unto those who are of the*
> *household of faith. Galatians 6:7-10*

This scripture tells us that we have a responsibility to reach out to those around us, especially to our spiritual brothers and sisters, and be faithful in administering the fruits of the Spirit. (The fruits of the Spirit are love, joy, peace, longsuffering, gentleness, goodness, faith, meekness and temperance.) When we are faithful in sharing these godly characteristics, God will see to it that the same things come back to us in the same propensity as we shared them. Likewise, if we sow the fruits of the flesh (such as adultery, fornication, uncleanness, lasciviousness, idolatry, witchcraft, hatred, variance, jealousies, wrath, strife, seditions, heresies, envyings, murders, drunkenness, and revellings), we will also receive these things in the same propensity as we gave them. It is very easy to see which list of fruits we should be displaying.

STAY FAITHFUL IN GIVING

This can be a major area of struggle and conflict when things are not going well in our lives. We must not love money or the things that money can buy. Rather, we need to appreciate money only for what we can do with it for the Kingdom of God.

> *Will a man rob God? Yet ye have robbed*
> *me. But ye say, Wherein have we robbed*
> *thee? In tithes and offerings. Ye are*
> *cursed with a curse: for ye have robbed*

me, even this whole nation. Bring ye all the tithes into the storehouse, that there may be meat in mine house, and prove me now herewith, saith the Lord of hosts, if I will not open you the windows of heaven, and pour you out a blessing, that there shall not be room enough to receive it. Malachi 3:8-10

He that giveth unto the poor shall not lack, but he that hideth his eyes shall have many a curse. Proverbs 28:27

He that hath pity upon the poor lendeth unto the LORD; and that which he hath given will he pay him again. Proverbs 19:17

Honor the Lord with thy substance, and with the first fruits of all thine increase; so shall thy barns be filled with plenty, and thy presses shall burst out with new wine. Proverbs 3:9-10

Love not the world, neither the things that are in the world. If any man love the world, the love of the Father is not in him. For all that is in the world, the lust of the flesh, and the lust of the eyes, and the pride of life, is not of the Father, but is of the world. 1 John 2:15-16

CHAPTER FOUR

STAY FAITHFUL TO MATE

If you are married and going through tough times, this is certainly *not* the time to let your eyes wander from your mate and start wondering whether you should split and go your separate ways. Cast aside any thoughts about what life might be like with someone else instead of your present mate. If you want to keep your marriage strong during times of testing and struggle, you must refuse to consider an easy-out solution. In marriage, you were joined together as a team with the Lord. Let the Holy Spirit bond you together as one. He alone can help you accomplish what you can never do in your own strength.

Husbands, love your wives, even as Christ also loved the church, and gave himself for it; ...so ought men to love their wives as their own bodies. He that loveth his wife loveth himself...For this cause shall a man leave his mother and father, and shall be joined unto his wife, and they two shall be one flesh... Nevertheless let everyone of you in particular so love his wife even as himself; and the wife see that she reverence her husband. Ephesians 5:25, 28, 31, 33

And did not He make one? Yet had he the residue of the spirit. And wherefore one? That He might seek a godly seed. Therefore take heed to your spirit, and let none deal treacherously against the wife of his youth. For the LORD, the God of

Israel, saith that He hateth putting away; for one covereth violence with his garment, saith the LORD of hosts: "Therefore take heed to your spirit, that ye deal not treacherously. Malachi 2:15-16

Likewise, ye husbands, dwell with your wives with understanding, giving honor unto the wife as unto the weaker vessel, and as being heirs together of the grace of life, that your prayers be not hindered. 1 Peter 3:7

God is clearly saying that He hates divorce. Wedding vows are never to be taken lightly, and lame excuses, public opinion, and tough times are not acceptable to God as justification for breaking them. The percentage of divorces experienced by born-again believers is shocking and embarrassing to God. Because of our lack of fidelity, we demonstrate that we're really no different than the rest of the world. We have no time for God's perfect plan. God did not create marriage to exist only as long as it was convenient. What God has joined together, let no man put asunder (Matthew 19:6). A successful marriage requires a total commitment to the other person, as well as total dependency upon God for strength to fulfill the vows in marriage. God hates divorce for good reason. Therefore, it must never be taken lightly by Christian believers.

Biblical Illustrations of Faith in Tough Times

GET UP AND GET GOING AGAIN

According to a statement made by Jesus in the Scriptures, the only way we will receive what we need in life is to *ask, seek and knock for it.* We must reach a point in our lives where we become aggressive instead of passive, a place where we desire, as well as expect, a change in our situation. "Status quo has got to go." We must get to a place in our lives where we just get *sick and tired of being sick and tired.* Jesus always stands ready to perform a miracle in our lives, something for which He has already paid the price. However, we must reach out to Him and take hold of it. We must appropriate it to our need in the same way that we receive our wonderful salvation. Jesus has already paid the price for *everything* that we will ever need in our lives. Consequently, there is nothing further that He needs to do. Everything is already in our account, and this account can never be overdrawn. We need only to act upon God's provision, by demonstrating faith in His Word. We must *expect* something to happen, because the special blessings of God usually don't automatically occur in our lives. Unless we utilize what God has provided, it does us no good. Ye have not because ye ask not. (James 4:2) God will never force us to receive His provision. It's like having money in the bank, and never using it.

I would like to highlight a number of very interesting incidents recorded in the Bible. These experiences provide relevant lessons for us today. The first incident is detailed in Matthew 14: 23-32.

WALKING ON THE WATER

One night, Jesus told His disciples to take the boat and go to the other side of the lake, while He spent time praying on the hillside. Jesus said that He would join them later. The disciples obeyed and sailed onto the currently-calm lake. After sailing for a short time, they suddenly found themselves in the middle of a ferocious storm, the kind of storm for which Lake Galilee was famous. The waves began splashing over the sides of the boat, threatening to capsize them. Though these men were expert fishermen and boatmen, they found themselves in a very perilous position. They applied the best of their human skill, training and experience to keep the sails in a good position to the wind, while fighting hard to keep the water bailed out of the boat. However, they found themselves quickly losing ground. The struggle lasted throughout the night, and it appeared the storm was going to win this battle and send them all to a premature, watery grave.

Suddenly, in the pitch of darkness, they saw Jesus walking toward them over the top of the stormy waves. The disciples weren't sure whether they were having hallucinations, or whether it really was Jesus coming to their assistance.

I find it very interesting that Jesus showed up at this particular point in their struggle. The hardest part of the battle is often at the darkest part of the night. My experience verifies that this is typical of Jesus. He usually shows up when it there is no apparent hope for survival, when life is at its very bleakest point, and all other options have fizzled. He comes on the scene when discouragement and total exhaustion are overwhelming, when we're convinced we can't hold on any longer.

The disciples were used to being on the water, as most of them had made their living on it before they joined Jesus' evangelistic team. However, this relentless storm had put a new respect in their hearts for the potential danger of the storms common to this lake. Any self-confidence they possessed about their abilities to cope with the power of nature was being severely tested. When all of their hope was depleted, Jesus appeared on the scene and came to them walking over the top of the *very same* water that was threatening to destroy their lives. Thus, Jesus was demonstrating that His power was superior over all the forces of nature. He was bigger than the storm, bigger than the waves, and bigger than the fear that was gripping their hearts. He certainly made His message clear to them.

Having Jesus walk on the water was one thing, but at this point, the story gets even crazier. Peter, one of the disciples in the boat, recognized that it was Jesus who was coming toward them. He impetuously stood up in the boat and called out, "If it be thou, Lord, bid me come unto thee on the water." He knew that Jesus was God. Therefore, He could do anything. Even the laws of nature were subservient to Jesus. Even though Peter's thought of walking on water was perhaps a bit grandiose, he wanted to make sure it *really was* the Lord out there. He also wanted to make double sure that his desire was something the Lord would totally approve. He wanted permission from Jesus to do what he wanted to accomplish. We have to give Peter *some* credit for not being *completely* crazy. Unless we know positively that the Lord is willing to authorize our desires, we can't be sure that He will help us achieve them. Thus, we need to be very, very sure that the Lord *is* the One really leading us, when we get inspired to step out in faith and do something for Him. We are well-assured that, if it is the Lord's will for us to do something, then He will enable us to accomplish it. Far too many Christians take off on ambitious plans, with only a casual presumption that this is what the Lord wants them to do. Then, when they make a mess of things, they can't figure out what went wrong, and why the Lord didn't show up to bail them out of their dilemma.

Though Peter got permission from Jesus to come to Him out on the water, Peter still had to be willing to take the next step. He had to stand up in that rocking, reeling boat and swing his legs out from the relative security of the boat. Then, he had to slide over the edge with his body, while hanging onto something as he dropped onto the water. He had to be willing to leave his comfort zone and venture into an unknown area with a questionable outcome. It appears he would have been a lot safer if he had stayed in the boat with the other disciples. The rest of the disciples were committed to that position, as none of them elected to join him on the water. In spite of the great gamble that he faced, Peter preferred to do the same thing that Jesus was doing, rather than remain in the rocking, reeling boat. In the meantime, the waves continued to splash over the sides of the boat, and the wind continued to scream and howl. This was not a fun-time scene. I've often wondered what the other disciples in the boat were thinking about, or hollering to Peter as he went over the edge. To everyone's amazement, a genuine miracle took place, as Peter didn't sink when his feet touched the water. Indeed, he *was* walking on the water, just as Jesus was doing. I don't know how far Peter walked, but the Scriptures are very clear that he *did do so.* He also walked in the right direction, because he walked toward Jesus. As long as he kept his eyes on Jesus, everything went just fine. For some strange reason, Peter then allowed his attention to be diverted. He obviously began thinking about the fact that what he was doing was completely impossible. Possibly he looked at the waves, and the inevitable quickly occurred. Peter possibly sank like a rock and desperately gasped for air, as water began filling his lungs. As he struggled in the raging water, at least he had the presence of mind to call out to Jesus to save him. Jesus simply reached out his hand, pulled Peter out of the water, and walked with him back to the boat. Peter did experience momentary failure, but the fact remains that he *did walk* on the water. The others who remained in the boat were only spectators to what Peter did. They never exercised the faith to attempt the same thing. Jesus gave Peter the desire of his heart, which was to do the same thing that Jesus was doing. No one could ever take away the reality of that experience from Peter, though he may have swallowed some water in the process.

A person who takes his eyes off Jesus, for even an instant, faces the same risk of failure that Peter did. Even our very best efforts will not be sufficient to keep us from sinking like a rock. It is always much easier to remain a spectator, pointing out what other people do wrong, than to focus upon the things they do right. Peter experienced a miracle when he listened to what the Lord told him to do, rather than listening to what the other disciples in the boat were saying. John 14:12 informs us that we can expect to do even greater things than Jesus did. It seems that Peter took the Lord's challenge seriously, and experienced one of the greatest thrills of his life. Peter's momentary failure did not occur because Jesus ran out of sufficient power to keep him afloat. Peter sank only because he took his eyes off Jesus and began to think about where *he* was and what *he* was doing. It is better to at least *attempt* to accomplish something worthwhile, even if it seems to be totally impossible to you or your most trusted advisors. You may experience some degree of failure, at least temporarily. Still, you will accomplish significantly more than those who are content to simply remain in their safety or comfort zone, just 'riding out the storm.'

FOUR HUNGRY LEPERS

The second interesting incident I'd like to comment on is recorded in II Kings 7:3-16. It's the story of four lepers who lived under very difficult circumstances. The city of

---

Samaria, where they lived, had been under a lengthy siege by an enemy army. All outside supplies were cut off. All citizens of the city were slowly starving to death, even to the point that mothers ate their newborn babies in order to keep themselves alive. Because of their disease, the four lepers were forced to live outside the city walls, totally unprotected from the enemy army. They were outcasts in their society. The people *inside* the walls were starving, so it takes little imagination to realize the plight of the four lepers *outside* the walls. The lepers had no other source of food. In sheer desperation one day, the starving, weak lepers looked at each other and their predicament and made a powerful statement. They said, "Why sit we here until we die?" They arrived at the realization that, if anything was going to change their situation, they needed to do something about it *themselves*. No one else appeared able to do anything about their circumsances, so they came to the conclusion that, *"If it's to be, it's up to me."* That marvelous revelation of truth needs to be applied to many people today as well. The lepers finally realized that, if they did nothing about their predicament, they were going to die. If they did *something*, there was at least a slim chance that their situation could change.

The wild idea these lepers got was almost as crazy as the one that Peter had. They decided the best course of action was to get up from their reclining position and head straight for the enemy's camp. In their weakened condition, their idea was preposterous. It would seem they should just get out of the area. However, they knew there was an ample supply of food at the enemy's camp. Somehow, emaciated as they were, they shuffled along the road, headed for the camp. God caused their movements to be amplified, so the enemy army believed a large opposing army was coming their way. Paranoia overwhelmed them so that their imaginations ran wild. Rather than prepare for battle against this apparent foe approaching their camp, they became irrational, and quickly abandoned the entire camp. The tough men of the army fled in all directions, never looking back, and left all of their provisions behind them. When the lepers arrived at the camp, they were overwhelmed at what they found. The first thing they did was sit down and gorge themselves on all of the wonderful food that was scattered about. Once their strength returned, they looked at each other and commented that this great abundance should be shared with their families, friends, and neighbors back in Samaria.

Four sick, feeble lepers were used mightily by God to bring havoc to an enemy's plans to destroy their city. When they got sick and tired of being sick and tired, they were able to bring deliverance to themselves as well as their city. Their own needs were met in great abundance, but so were the needs of an entire city abundantly met, as God's blessing was overwhelming. Like the desperate situation these lepers faced, so many people today face severely trying circumstances. They need to quit waiting for someone else to do something about their lot in life. They must get up from their reclining positions and step out with faith in a big God, to see what He will do to change things for them. Instead of waiting for the federal government, the local church, the county welfare program, a wealthy family, or sympathetic friends to come to their aid, it may be time for *them* to get up and get moving. Then they need to allow the Holy Spirit to provide direction and wisdom, so they can be led to his miraculous and bountiful provision. No one can predict how things will turn out once a journey of faith is started, but it is pretty easy to predict the outcome of doing *nothing*, hoping someone *else* will do something.

The only people who *never* make mistakes are the people who never *do* anything. We need to be ready and willing to allow the Lord to lead us in a course of action that will change, not only *our* situation, but also the situations of others around us. That will never happen until we are willing to take chances and step out beyond our comfort zones. We need to stretch beyond where we *have* been and what we *have* known, and allow God to do the things that only *He* can do in our lives.

A BIG ASSIGNMENT

Another example of someone willing to get out of a comfort zone and let God work a miracle in her life is the story of Mary, the mother of Jesus. One day an angel approached her, informing her that she had been chosen for the special task of being the birth mother of the Messiah. She likely had many questions about how she'd explain this to her parents and Joseph. However, before those questions were answered, she simply responded to the angel's announcement, "Behold the handmaid of the LORD. Be it unto me according to your will."

I have heard myself praying a similar prayer many times. I tell the Lord that I am willing to do whatever He asks of me, even if it makes no sense to me or to anyone else. I don't want to be concerned with whether I look ridiculous or crazy. Being in the center of God's perfect will for my life is the only thing that is worth living or dying for.

There will always be the possibility of failure and "loss of face" when we move away from our comfort zone and fully trust the Lord to work things out in our lives, in His way, in His time. I doubt Peter, the four lepers or Mary ever regretted doing what they did, though others who observed them would likely have thought they were completely out of their minds. Peter eventually went to his grave knowing that he had indeed walked on the water, though he possibly ended up drinking some of it. The other disciples in the boat could only talk of someone else's experience. The four lepers eventually died, remembering how God had used them to end the famine and deliver their city from their enemy's siege. The other citizens could only recall someone else's experience of trusting God in a time of crisis to bring about a miracle of deliverance. Mary went to her eternal reward, knowing that God had miraculously used her to bring the Messiah to earth. Obedience to what God is calling and leading us to do will cause not only our needs to be met, but also those of others. God will never lead us where His grace cannot sustain us.

Can you imagine how God might want to have *you* stretch beyond your comfort zones so you are available to Him? Then He can accomplish something supernatural and marvelous through *you*. Why continue to be content in your miserable state of affairs, watching God do marvelous things with and for *other* people? Don't be afraid of making mistakes. Just don't sit around playing it safe, never taking a chance, wondering why God or somebody else doesn't do something to drop a miracle in your lap and keep the stress level down in your life.

THE DEATH OF A CHILD

I am reminded of a major crisis in the life of King David, as recorded in II Samuel 12. The baby born to Bathsheba and him, as the result of their adultery, had become gravely ill. Nathan, the prophet, had predicted the baby would die, as evidence of God's punishment upon them for their sin. Still, David earnestly fasted and prayed to the Lord for a miracle that would spare the baby's life. He begged God to be merciful. Many of David's personal staff members at the palace accompanied him in this effort. Still, the baby quit breathing.

Because David was in such agony of spirit, the others feared telling David the bad news, thinking he would do something irrational. David soon detected the change in their countenances, and knew that something serious had happened. He simply asked, "Is the baby dead?" When they confirmed his suspicions, David responded to the bad news by getting up from his place of prayer, washing his face, changing his clothes of mourning, and looking for something to eat. The others questioned his radical transformation, and David simply responded, "I shall go to him, but he shall not return to me." David demonstrated faith and hope in His God, as well as complete acceptance of God's will.

Only those who have faith in the promise of God know confidently that there really *is* a place called heaven, and they can have true peace when standing by the open grave of a loved one. They anticipate a reunion with their loved one someday, as long as the deceased had a relationship with the Lord while alive. They are assured that God will someday make everything understandable. Therefore, they are better able to accept their present loss. They still mourn, but their mourning is different from the mourning of those without this hope. They can still sing and be happy, in spite of their great loss, because they believe their loved one is already in God's presence. They know their loved one is much better off. This special "joy of the Lord" that believers have at such times is a *real* commodity. It is not a "pie in the sky by and by" pipe dream, as scoffers would have us believe.

David knew he had done everything he could to keep his baby alive. Now it was time to pick up the pieces and move on with living. *Everyone* must do likewise in times of grief and sorrow, though most of us find that our recovery period is a bit longer than David's was.

This story of David reminds me of a special song I have sung or played at many funerals.

GOING HOME
Bill Gaither
copyrighted William J. Gaither

Many times in my childhood when we'd travel so far;
By nightfall how weary I'd grow;

Father's arm would slip 'round me
So gently He'd say, "my child, we're going home."
Now the twilight is fading and the day soon shall end;
I get homesick the farther I roam;
But my father has led me each step of the way;
And now we are going home.

Oh my heart gets so heavy and I'm longing to see
All my loved ones and friends I have known;
Every step draws me nearer to the land of my dreams,
Praise God, I'm going home.

Chorus—
Going home, I'm going home.
There's nothing to hold me here;
Well, I've caught a glimpse of that Heavenly land,
Praise God, I am going home.

A WIDOW'S PLIGHT

Let's consider the story of Elijah and the widow from Zarapheth, as recorded in I Kings 17:7-16. Elijah, the man of God, was on the run from an evil king, Ahab, who wanted to kill him. Elijah had promised the king that the nation would experience a time of drought, as punishment from God, because the king was so evil. When the drought became reality, Ahab tried to blame Elijah for it, and threatened to kill him. Elijah went into seclusion for a period of time, and God used the ravens to bring his daily meals to him, as he hid alongside a creek in the wilderness. Eventually, the creek dried up because of the drought, and Elijah was forced to move on because the ravens no longer showed up at mealtime. This is another example of someone being used of God in his generation, but still not being exempt from experiencing some tough times and adjustments in his own life. As Elijah hungrily approached the village of Zarapheth that afternoon, he encountered a widow gathering firewood. He felt impressed of the Holy Spirit to initiate a casual conversation with her. He learned that she was a very poor widow and that she had a son. Because of the terrible famine, she was gathering firewood that day so she could take it home and prepare the last portion of flour in her meal barrel for a final meal for herself and her son. There would be no remaining option for the two of them after that meal, except to surrender to the inevitable fate of death by starvation. Things looked very bleak. Even a veritable optimist would have a tough time finding something positive about this set of circumstances.

In response to the story of her desperate plight, Elijah, the man of God, the man who was living by faith himself, made a seemingly unreasonable request of her. He requested that she fix *him* a meal *first* from her limited food supply. The widow must have looked askance at him, to be sure that she had heard him correctly. Nevertheless, she sensed a spark of faith in her heart, because she recognized him as a man of God. He had told her to not be afraid, but to grant his request. He didn't offer any promise that something good would happen to her, just because she met his need.

There's no way this request could have made sense to the natural, human mind. Sometimes, it is better not to spend too much time pondering decisions regarding faith issues, especially in the light of desperate, personal need. There definitely are times when we just need to take a "leap of faith," knowing that the Lord can amply meet every personal need. He notes our immediate obedience, knowing full well what that obedience is costing us personally. He will not ask us to make unreasonable sacrifices, except when He wants to move us to the next level of faith. He wants to teach us more of His sufficient grace and miraculous provision. Those experiences will always lead to rejoicing over how God supplies the personal need.

Without any further contemplation, the widow took a major step of faith and proceeded to prepare Elijah the requested meal, which he promptly consumed with thanksgiving. After cleaning up the table and doing the dishes, she went back to her "empty" meal barrel to take another look, not knowing just what to expect. Surprisingly, it wasn't empty, but there was enough flour remaining in the barrel for her to fix two more meals. How could she have previously overlooked this flour? Soon their stomachs were full also, and they rejoiced in God's provision.

The next day, she decided to check the meal barrel again, and there was still enough left so she could fix meals for Elijah, her son and herself. Because this widow put someone else's need ahead of her own very desperate one, God honored her faith and saw to it that she always had enough for three more meals. The next day there was still just enough for three more meals. Though the famine continued for several more months, she never ran out of flour in her barrel. I've always wondered why God didn't just fill the barrel for her so she wouldn't have to keep checking the barrel. The important issue is that God met her need every day, just three meals at a time, because that is all she really needed. God rewarded her initial obedience and faith, and she didn't really need a *full* barrel. God will never abandon people of faith when they move in obedience to the Holy Spirit during times of crisis and great need, rather than relying on their own human logic and understanding. Human logic and understanding will deny us the opportunity to see what God can do about our situation. He will turn the challenge that comes to test our faith into an exciting opportunity to experience His miraculous provision. The widow was very grateful that she had been given the wonderful opportunity of being a blessing to Elijah, the man of God. She and her son would have died of starvation if they hadn't responded in obedience to Elijah's challenge to her faith.

My personal experience tells me that God often works this way today. God may choose to provide a miracle of healing for us about the same time we are praying a prayer of faith for someone else's healing. God may use someone else to win our children to the Lord, in response to our reaching out to someone else's wayward children. God can still bring healing to our own broken marriage when we reach out to minister love to someone else whose marriage is in trouble. We must not sit around thinking that we are the only ones with problems and needs. Neither should we think that we can be used of God to meet other people's needs *only* after our own needs are fully met. If that were the case, most of us would never be privileged to be a blessing to someone else, because we will never *get* to that point. Like the widow's meal barrel, our barrel may never be full either, but that must not stop us from ministering first to someone else in need. The choice is ours. We can make the experiences in our lives into stepping stones or into stumbling blocks and tombstones. We can become either bitter or better. Which will it be?

A FAMILY TORN APART BY JEALOUSY

I often recall another story of great faith, recorded in the Old Testament. It is the story of Joseph, told in the book of Genesis. His family had been bitterly torn apart because of jealousy and multiple misunderstandings with his brothers. Simply put, Joseph's brothers hated him. As a result, Joseph was overpowered by his brothers one day. They sold him to some traveling slave traders, who took him to Egypt and resold him at an auction. In the meantime, his brothers took the beautiful coat which his father had given him, and smeared animal blood on it. They took it to their father and told him that they found the coat in the wilderness. They said Joseph had obviously been killed by a wild animal, and this was all that was left of him. The shock nearly killed Joseph's father, and he grieved bitterly for many years, never suspecting that his other children had lied to him.

When Joseph was auctioned as a slave, he was acquired by one of the political leaders of Egypt. His new master was very impressed by his talents, and soon gave him complete reign over his household affairs. However, the master's wife saw what a handsome young man Joseph was, and tried to entice Joseph to have sex with her. He persistently refused her temptation, knowing God would not approve of this conduct. He loved God and was committed to a life of sexual purity. However, she was not to be put off so easily. One day she caught him alone in the house and grabbed him by his jacket. She pleaded with him to come to bed with her, but Joseph jerked away. He left his jacket in her hands, as he fled from the house. The woman started yelling "rape, rape," as the other servants returned to the house. She told them that Joseph had tried to rape her. When the news reached Joseph's master, he believed his wife's version of the story. Though Joseph was innocent, he was the victim of false accusation. As a slave, his story did not have much credibility, and he was sentenced to spend time in prison.

Time passed. Though Joseph was in prison, God did not forget about him. Because of his consistent good conduct, the head prison guard eventually elevated him to the position of trustee. Though he remained a prisoner, Joseph maintained a good mental attitude and worked hard at his assigned tasks. Meanwhile, everyone else forgot about him. One day God used him to interpret two different dreams that two new inmates had the previous night. Both of Joseph's interpretations were fulfilled the next day, exactly as he had predicted. One prisoner was executed, and the other was restored to his position with the Pharaoh. The restored servant faithfully promised Joseph

---

that he would plead Joseph's case to the king at the earliest possible opportunity. However, in the midst of all his excitement at being restored to his former position, he forgot to keep his promise.

Having to deal with injustices like this, Joseph certainly had many opportunities to become bitter and disillusioned. God had given Joseph many promises during his youth, but He hadn't told him there would be all these difficult years of slavery and imprisonment before the promises could be fulfilled. Nevertheless, Joseph's attitude remained very positive, and he refused to become bitter over the unfair way he had been treated by his brothers, his master and his fellow inmates. He knew that God was still in absolute control over every circumstance in his life, and that His promises would surely be fulfilled when He was ready. This type of experience separates those who have faith in a loving, all-powerful God from those who only serve God when it is convenient, or when everything is going just great in their lives.

My favorite portion of Joseph's story is told a few chapters later, after God used him to interpret a dream that the Pharaoh of Egypt had. No one was able to interpret the dream. Then Pharaoh's servant, the ex-prisoner whose dream had been correctly interpreted by Joseph, suddenly remembered his promise to Joseph to talk to Pharaoh about him. He spoke to Pharaoh, who immediately sent for him in prison. Because God had prepared Joseph to be just the right place at just the right time, Joseph quickly interpreted Pharaoh's dream and was rapidly elevated to the position of vice-pharaoh of Egypt. His primary duty was to specifically prepare the country for the impending famine predicted in the king's dream that Joseph had interpreted.

When the famine arrived seven years later as predicted, it affected all of Egypt, as well as the country where Joseph's father and his brothers still lived. When their families got short on food, Joseph's father instructed his sons to travel to Egypt to buy food. He had heard that Egypt still had food, and was willing to sell it. Egypt's abundant food supply was stored in the warehouses that Joseph had established, in response to the king's command. Joseph's brothers were unaware that he was even alive, let alone in such a position of authority in Egypt. When they arrived in Egypt, the very person they needed to contact to buy the needed food supplies, was none other than Joseph. He recognized them immediately, but they didn't have any idea they were dealing with their brother, the one they had sold into slavery many years previously. They purchased their food supplies and returned home. Once there, they were very surprised when they opened their sacks of grain, and found that the money they had paid for the grain was still in their sacks. They didn't know what to make of this, but they were very glad to be back home.

Sometime later, as the famine persisted, they began to run low on food again, and their father requested the brothers make a second trip to Egypt to buy food. It was on this trip that Joseph finally told his brothers who he was. Initially, they were severely frightened, thinking this was Joseph's opportunity to get back at them for the cruel way that they treated him. However, Joseph simply responded that what had been meant for evil, God had turned into good. He recognized that the dreams God had given him as a child had now been fulfilled, though it had been a long, hard road from his boyhood home. God had not failed him. Everything he had endured had simply prepared him for the position of trust and power he now held. He quickly forgave his brothers their misdeeds, and their relationship was restored. Because there were still several years of famine ahead, Joseph invited his brothers to bring their father and the rest of the family to Egypt, where they could have better access to a food supply. In God's wisdom and timing, none of this could have happened if Joseph hadn't been sent to Egypt many years earlier, and prepared through many hardships to be in the right place at the right time, when God needed him to do something special for Him. God had also known, all along, that the Israelites would be caught in the pending famine, and that they would need to be temporarily relocated so they wouldn't starve. He had simply sent Joseph to Egypt, in a roundabout way, ahead of time, to prepare for their arrival. If Joseph hadn't been who, where, and what he was at the time, the story would have a much different ending.

There are so many times in life when it seems that evil has the upper hand, that God has lost control of the affairs in our lives. It is so hard to remain positive and patient so that God can work all of the details out for a miracle to take place. If Joseph had allowed himself to become bitter, or if he had grown exasperated with the seemingly endless delay, he would have missed out on all that God wanted to do with him. He would never have been elevated to the position of power and prestige that he achieved. He would never have experienced the better solution of letting God take care of those who had mistreated him, instead of his trying to get even with them. He would never have been in the right place at the right time to accomplish what God had in mind for the nation of Israel.

In the midst of a struggle and the despair of thinking that even God could never get your mess straightened out, try singing this song.

> ## GOD'S NOT THROUGH BLESSING YOU
> *Mike Murdock*
>
> A man lost every dime to his name,
> His best friends even said he was through.
> But God said, "Job, your best days are just ahead,
> 'Cause I'm not through blessing you."
>
> Have you ever prayed for something, day after day,
> And nothing happened?
> Have you ever asked God for a miracle
> and it seemed the answer would never come?
> That very moment, that very second,
> you might feel like letting go, quitting,
> You may not realize it, friend,
> but you might just be a moment from your miracle.
> Don't quit, don't let go,
> 'Cause God's not through blessing you.

> God's not through blessing you.
> God's not through blessing you.
> Never give up, what He says He will do.
> God's not through blessing you.

A TRIAL OF FIRE

Another inspiring Old Testament story recorded in Daniel 3:1-29 is that of Shadrach, Meshach and Abednego, the three Jewish young men who were captured during an invasion of Israel, and taken as slaves to Persia. As the story goes, the King of Persia commissioned a huge statue of himself to be erected. At the dedication ceremony, he commanded all the inhabitants of Persia to bow down and worship the statue. Shadrach, Meshach and Abednego were believers in God. They knew they couldn't obey this command and still remain true to their God. Though everyone else around them bowed in worship to the statue, they held to their convictions and remained standing. They told the king that their God was *able* to deliver them from his hand, but if He chose not to, they still *not* bow down to his statue. They knew their disobedience was going to be severely challenged, because the king did not have a very good sense of humor. He gave them another chance to change their minds and bow before his statue. When they still refused, he had them bound hand and foot with tight ropes, and thrown into a furnace that had been heated to seven times its normal temperature. The fire was so hot that even the soldiers who threw them into the furnace were incinerated at the door as they obeyed this merciless king. As the boys fell into the pit of the blazing furnace, the fire quickly burned their ropes asunder. However, instead of being burned to a crisp, they found themselves free to walk around inside the furnace, unharmed by the flames. The same flames which were intended to incinerate them, instantly set them free. The king's mouth dropped open in amazement, as he observed this unexpected outcome. He also noticed that a fourth person appeared to be accompanying them as they walked around in the midst of the raging flames. That person appeared to be the Son of God. I have an idea that they were not just walking around in the furnace. I rather think they were singing a song of deliverance and victory, dancing amidst the flames and worshipping the mighty God who was big enough to rescue them from this major testing of their faith. The king beckoned for them to come out of the furnace, and when they did, he noticed there was not even the smell of smoke on them. He immediately declared that the God these young men served was to be honored by all the people of Persia, and there was no more talk about bowing down before his statue. What an exciting way for these three friends to spend an afternoon! The fiery trial of their faith didn't turn out to be such a bad experience after all. Most of us would much prefer that God not allow us to go through the trial by fire, that He would simply deliver us beforehand. However, sometimes God wants us to experience the fire, which in turn provides the needed deliverance for us. In fact, it provided a powerful testimony to these men of how the God they served was able to deliver them *through* the fire, even though He chose not to deliver them *from* the fire. Faith in our all-powerful God is built and strengthened primarily because we successfully survive the trials and tribulations we encounter, not because we avoid them.

Just as Jesus was with *them* at the time of their crisis, so we know that He will be with *us* in the midst of whatever trial or testing we might experience. We don't see Him physically, but we will always be able to sense His presence. Those who observe us in our dilemma will likely see the evidence of His presence in us as well. The fire that was intended to end the lives of these three young men, only served to free them from the tight ropes that bound them. They were able to testify to the greatness of their God, and the entire country took note. Any worry or fretting they might have done about the outcome of this incident, was entirely futile. God had promised that they would go *through* the fire and come out successfully on the other side, and not just *into* the fire to die.

This is another very special song that I love to sing.

SHELTERED IN THE ARMS OF GOD
Dottie Rambo and Jimmie Davis
Copyrighted, but unverified

I feel the touch of hand so kind and tender.
They're leading me in paths that I must trod;
I have no fear when Jesus walks beside me,
For I'm sheltered in the arms of God.

Soon I shall hear the call from Heaven's portals
"Come home, my child, it's the last mile you must trod;"
I'll fall a sleep and wake in God's new Heaven,

Sheltered safe within the arms of God

Chorus—
So let the storms rage high, the dark clouds rise,
They won't worry me,
For I'm sheltered safe within the arms of God;
He walks with me, and naught of earth shall harm me,
For I'm sheltered in the arms of God.

Fear thou not; for I am with thee: be not dismayed: for I am thy God: I will strengthen thee; yea, I will help thee; yea, I will uphold thee with the right hand of my righteousness. Isaiah 41:10

Casting all your cares upon him; for he careth for you. 1 Peter 5:7

Be anxious for nothing, but in everything by prayer and supplication with thanksgiving, let your requests be made known unto God. Philippians 4:6

I include the words from another grand old hymn of the church, another one that we sang at my son's funeral October 17, 1995.

DOES JESUS CARE?
Frank E. Graeff/Lincoln J. Hall
(public domain)

Does Jesus care when my heart is pained,
Too deeply for mirth and song?
As the burdens press, and the cares distress,
And the way grows weary and long.

Does Jesus care when my way is dark,
With a nameless dread and fear?
As the day fades into deep night shades,
Does He care enough to be near?

Does Jesus care when I've tried and failed,
To resist some temptation strong?
When for my deep grief I find no relief,
Though my tears flow all the night long?

Does Jesus care when I've said good-by
To the dearest on earth to me?
And my sad heart aches, till it nearly breaks,
Is it aught to Him, does He care?

Chorus—
Oh, yes He cares, I knows He cares.
His heart is touched with my grief.
When the days are weary, the long nights dreary,
I know my Savior cares.

This is an appropriate place to share the words to this very special song that I have loved for many years.

SOMETHING WORTH LIVING FOR
Words by Doug Oldham
Music by Bill Gaither,
copyright 1967, William J. Gaither

Life was shattered and hope was gone
Crushing the load that I bore;
Then out of the depths I cried, O God,
Give me something worth living for.

There, with life at it's lowest ebb
Who could heal and restore?
Then He came and mended my broken heart,
He gave me something worth living for.

O, the joy of sins forgiv'n,
There's nothing the same as before.
My life overflows since Jesus came
And gave me something worth living for.

Chorus—
Something more than my yesterdays
More than I had before,
Something more than wealth or fame,
He gave me something worth living for.

THINGS TO AVOID

Up to this point, I have been sharing with you many positive activities a Christian *should* focus upon when major tragedy or complicated problems come along. However, there are also some things that we must make sure that we do *not* allow ourselves to do. From my personal observation and experience, I want to bring into focus the activities we must *avoid*. Some of our responses are automatic, natural reactions to certain dilemmas. We must make certain that these natural responses do not short-circuit God's ability to intervene and help us in our crisis. This can certainly happen if we allow ourselves to express the wrong attitude or the wrong response during tough times. This list of things *not* to do is not intended to be all-inclusive, but it is very important to note whether any of the following responses or reactions is typical of us. Only when we acknowledge our errors can we make the necessary correction, with the Lord's help, so we don't hamstring God from doing what He wants to bring us through the problem and into complete victory.

DON'T PANIC OR DESPAIR

It is so easy to get uptight, become paranoid and think that the very worst possible thing is going to happen to us. Because we choose to focus upon the things that are going wrong instead of going right, we can't get a clear picture of what is really happening. Thus, we grasp desperately for sundry solutions with our foggy understanding. Our natural reaction is to panic and lose hope for a better day. Therefore, we must counter this reaction by reminding ourselves *that God is still on the throne. He is still in control. He is still bigger than Satan. He will never leave us alone or fail* us. We must refuse to let the enemy of our souls lie to us about God's intense interest in our personal welfare, or about His ability to successfully deal with every one of our circumstances. That is why we must learn to *wait upon the Lord* and *wait for the Lord* as never before. If we lean upon our own finite wisdom and human strength in an attempt to resolve the matter, we only make matters worse. God knows everything there is to know about the problem, and He *alone* knows how to work out all of the details for our best interest. When difficult times come, God has the perfect opportunity to demonstrate how loving, kind, wise, and powerful *He* really is. He knows how to bring us through every tough time in life. John 10:10 reminds us that the "thief cometh but to steal, and to kill, and to destroy: I am come that they might have life, and that they might have it more abundantly." From this Scripture, it is easy to understand that the devil is very bad and that God is very good. James 1:17 confirms that "every good and every perfect gift is from above, and cometh down from the Father of lights, with whom is no variableness, neither shadow of turning." The good things always come from our Lord, and the bad things come from our enemy. Once we have that key principle figured out, we are better prepared to realize that, through Christ, we really *are* more than conquerors. (Romans 8:37) Instead of sitting around 'singing the blues' about our situation, we could better focus upon singing songs like:

JESUS NEVER FAILS
Arthur A. Luther, copyright 1927
Singspiration Music

Earthly friends may prove untrue,
Doubts and fears assail.
One still loves and cares for you,
Jesus never fails.

Tho' the sky be dark and drear,
Fierce and strong the gale.
Just remember He is near,
And He never fails.

In life's dark and bitter hour,
Love will still prevail.
Trust His everlasting pow'r,
Jesus will not fail.

Chorus—
Jesus never fails.
Jesus never fails.
Heav'n and earth may pass away,
But Jesus never fails.

Or this song:

THE WORLD DIDN'T GIVE IT TO ME
*Gary S. Paxton and William J. and
Gloria Gaither, copyright 1976, 1977,
Christian Grit Music Press*

This smile on my face wasn't always there
'cause troubles used to get me down,
Hassles and problems from ev'ry direction
Used to make me wear a frown;
In the midst of the storms I found a deep
contentment
To help me face each night and day;
You see, the world didn't give it to me,
And the world can't take it away.

This steppin' round light in my feet that you
see
Wasn't always lively and light;
But when Jesus picked me up and started
melodies ringin'
They always come out happy and bright.
All I have to do is keep on lookin' at Him;
Follow, trust and then obey,
Because the world didn't give it to me
And the world can't take it away.

Let me tell you ' bout the treasure and
possessions I came into
When I put Him on the throne of my life:
A conscience that's clear and a fam'ly that
loves me,
An antidote for heartache and strife.
The world always says that you can't take it

with you;
But my riches transfer okay,
'cause the world didn't give it to me
And the world can't take it away.

Chorus—
The world didn't give it to me, and the world
can't take it away.
The world didn't give it to me and the world
can't take it away.
This happy face that I'm wearing, you know
my Jesus put it there to stay.
And since the world didn't give it to me, I
said the world can't take it away.

DON'T LET THE ENEMY ROB YOU

It is amazing how the Lord will use the personal
testimony of the personal, painful experiences we
successfully overcome, with His help, to bless and
encourage others. He helps us make a positive impact on
them when we share our stories of how He helped us cope
during times of trials and tribulations. Our testimony will
have far greater effectiveness and credibility than mere
theory or "pie-in-the-sky by and by" logic will ever have.
Our personal experience of God's mighty power will
carry more weight with other hurting people than simply
quoting Scripture verses or reading someone else's
comments from another popular book. There is more
significant credibility because it is something we have
lived, not something we memorized or heard someone
else say. God wants to make something beautiful out of

our pain and scars, if we will just let Him do it. God is not through blessing us or using us, though it may seem at times that He is a million miles away and our prayers are not getting through at all.

A statement I've heard many times, and which is credited to Mike Murdock, a Bible teacher I love to watch on Christian TV, states that what we make happen for others, God will also make happen for us. In other words, God will often act to meet our own needs shortly after we allow Him to use us as a blessing to others. That is why it is so important to always remain available to God, regardless of what might be happening in our own lives. He'll not overlook the fact that we also have unmet needs.

DON'T LOOK FOR 'QUICK-FIX 'ANSWERS

One of our main faults, as humans, is that we possess very little natural patience and very little perspective on the big picture. We want things to happen right now, and the sooner the better. We dislike dealing with the uncertainties of the unknown, as well as the unexpected. We are uncomfortable unless we can see the end from the beginning, the future from the vantage of today. However, the more you understand about God, the more you realize that God does not operate on our high-intensity timetables. He alone can see the end from the beginning, and He will not get high blood pressure or nurse an ulcer over problems that appear to have no foreseeable solution. Even in the midst of a most urgent matter, God always knows how to keep things under His perfect control. His ways and timing will always bring about the best solution at exactly the right time.

Therefore, God is unlikely to supply an urgent financial need by causing you to win a current sweepstakes promotion, even if you received a confirmation letter declaring that you are entered in the final drawing. God's ways of provision are far superior to those of this world. The same holds true for your chances of winning the current lottery drawing, or any other "get-rich-quick" scheme that regularly comes your way. About the time you think you've heard about every scheme there is, another friend or casual acquaintance calls you with a personal invitation to attend a "wonderful opportunity meeting" some evening at a local restaurant or hotel. Usually, very little information is given regarding the nature of the meeting, but once you arrive, the program for the evening is focused upon getting you to invest your time and money. The more you have available, the better. Then you can get in on the "ground floor" of another low-risk, sure-fire program geared to stimulate your greed and theirs. You are told it will ultimately solve all of your financial problems. The major key to success in this business is that you recruit as many others as you can, as quickly as you can. Many of God's people have spent untold effort, time and money trying to get rich quickly, pursuing an endless list of multi-level marketing plans which distribute products or services of every imaginable shape, size and color, usually at considerably marked-up prices. Though often touted as being "God-ordained" by their promoters, Christians need to be very cautious about them. We must be sure our motives are pure, and that God is indeed directing our steps in these decisions. We must be very sure we are hearing His voice, not that of someone trying to con us into something, hoping to capitalize on our time, ability and money.

If you are lonely, it unlikely God is going to lead you to the nearest bar in order to introduce you to a new friend. He is not likely to bring you a new companion by leading you to place a singles ad in the newspaper, or by leading you to Internet chat rooms. God is fully aware of your present circumstances, and I can personally attest to how quickly He can bring the perfect companion to you at the perfect time (more on that later!). His ways will always lead you into holiness and purity, and you will never have any reason to be ashamed, embarrassed, or regretful over your actions or decisions.

If you need a new job, it is unlikely you will have to resort to illegal activities to better yourself. You can be sure He will *not* lead you into a situation where you have to compromise your morals or convictions. You won't need to cut corners, use bribes, or pay someone 'under the table' to get the job God wants you to have. He gave you your talents. He knows how to direct your steps to bring you to the right place at the right time, so that your needs can be met abundantly and you can be an asset to the Kingdom of God.

God is still God, and He doesn't need to resort to the ways of this world to accomplish His will. We just need to trust Him completely. He can be counted on to bring us through each crisis situation we encounter, victoriously. However, He will do it in *His* time and in *His* way.

> *Take heed, and beware of covetousness:*
> *for a man's life consisteth not in the*
> *abundance of the things which he*
> *possesseth. Luke 12:15*

Another great song of surrender to sing at times like this is...

HAVE THINE OWN WAY
Adelaide A. Pollard/George C. Stebbins, (public domain)
copyright 1907, renewed 1935

Have Thine own way, Lord. Have Thine own way.
Thou art the potter, I am the clay.
Mold me and make me after thy will,
While I am waiting, yielded and still.

Have Thine own way, Lord. Have Thine own way.
Search me and try me, Master, today.
Whiter than snow, Lord, wash me just now,
As in Thy presence, humbly I bow.

Have Thine own way, Lord. Have Thine own way.
Wounded and weary, help me I pray
Power, all power surely in Thine.
Touch me and heal me, Savior divine.

Have Thine own way, Lord. Have Thine own way.

Hold o'er my being absolute sway.
Fill with Thy Spirit till all shall see,
Christ only always, living in me.

DON'T LET CIRCUMSTANCES RUN YOU

It is so easy to let things get out of focus when problems of life pile up on us. We can't see the forest for the trees. The result is that we get "tunnel vision." We can't see the full picture. If we take a quarter and hold it at a distance in front of us, we will certainly see the quarter, but we will also see everything else that is out in front of us. However, if we move the quarter right up close to the eye, everything else is blocked out, and we see only the quarter. If we allow ourselves to have tunnel vision, we find ourselves focusing only on the problem, not the solution. The problem becomes so large we see nothing else. With God's help, we need to step back far enough from our problem so we can see the situation through God's eyes, instead of our own. God always sees the full picture, and knows exactly the best method or choice for us. Therefore, He can direct us to the best solution or alternative. God never gets painted into a corner by circumstances so that He is left with no way out of the dilemma. There is *always* a way through any situation. We've got to believe that. There is always a way under, a way through, or a way around the problem. God is still in the miracle-working business, just as He demonstrated in the Bible.

> *I will lift up mine eyes unto the hills, from whence cometh my help. Psalms 121:1*

> *And call upon me in the day of trouble: I will deliver thee, and thou shalt glorify me. Psalm 50:15*

This newer worship song helps keep things in perspective also:

AWESOME GOD
Rich Mullins, copyright 1988
BMG Songs, Inc.

When He rolls up His sleeves He ain't just puttin' on the ritz;
Our God is an awesome God.
There is thunder in His footsteps and lightening in His fists;
Our God is an awesome God.
And the Lord wasn't jokin' when He kicked 'em out of Eden;
It wasn't for no reason that He shed His blood.
His return is very soon and so you better be believin'
That our God is an awesome God.

But when the sky was starless in the void of the night;
Our God is an awesome God.
He spoke into the darkness and created the light;
Our God is an awesome God.
The judgment and wrath He poured out on

Sodom;
The mercy and grace He gave us at the cross.
I hope that we have not too quickly forgotten that
Our God is an awesome God.

Chorus—
Our God is an awesome God.
He reigns from Heaven above;
With wisdom, pow'r, and love.
Our God is an awesome God.

Keeping our focus upon a super-big God will keep the problem from getting bigger than it really is. It is true that, in times of severe crisis, the dilemma can appear quite massive. Especially at times like that, we must keep our focus upon the Lord. Only *He* is bigger than whatever mountain is standing in our way, blocking our vision, keeping us from experiencing the blessings or victory God has prepared for us. .

> *If ye have faith as a grain of mustard seed, ye shall say unto this mountain, remove hence to yonder place; and it shall remove; and nothing shall be impossible unto you." Matthew 17:20*

DON'T COWER BEFORE THE ENEMY

We need to remind ourselves, from time to time, just who we really are in Christ Jesus. If we are believers, the Bible declares that we are children of God, joint-heirs with Jesus Christ, conquerors, promise keepers, and people in whom the presence and the anointing of God dwells. Therefore, we are winners, not losers. We are overcomers though Christ who strengthens us. The final chapter for our lives on this earth has already been written, and we already know how it will end. We already know who wins the battle. There is no need for us to live in fear and trepidation, overcome with desperation and despair. Remember, our enemy is nothing but a liar. He can't really hurt us. His doom has already been determined. God votes for us. Satan votes against us. How we cast our vote determines a majority vote as well as the outcome of the election.

Finally, my brethren, be strong in the Lord and in the power of His might. Put on the whole armor of God, that ye may be able to stand against the wiles of the devil. For we wrestle not against flesh and blood, but against principalities, against powers, against the rulers of the darkness of this world, against spiritual wickedness in high places. Therefore, take unto you the whole armor of God, that ye may be able to withstand in the evil day and, having done all, to stand. Stand therefore, having your loins girded about with truth, and having on the breastplate of righteousness, and your feet shod with the preparation of the Gospel of peace. Above all, take the shield of faith, wherewith ye shall be able to quench all the fiery darts of the wicked. And take the helmet of salvation and the sword of the Spirit, which is the Word of God, praying always with all prayer and supplication in the Spirit, and watching thereunto with all perseverance and supplication for all saints. Ephesians 6:11-18

Well, Hallelujah! This doesn't sound like God has called us to be part of any "second-rate" outfit. We don't need to apologize for who we are in Christ Jesus. We don't need to run and hide from our enemy when he attacks. We don't need to wonder about what God is going to do to defeat the enemy. It has already been determined that God and His people are destined to win, and that Satan is *already* defeated. The battle is *already* won. *Praise the Lord.*

This is another great song to sing in the midst of a great battle...

I'M A CONQUEROR
 Shirley Powell, copyright 1977
 Scripture In Song

I'm a conqueror and victorious.
I'm reigning with Jesus.
I'm seated in Heavenly places with Him,

with Him.
For the Kingdom of God is within me.
I know no defeat — only victory.
For the Kingdom of God is within me.
I know no defeat, only strength and power.

DON'T TELL GOD HOW TO SOLVE IT

God's ways and thoughts are always so much higher than ours. We simply need to draw so close to Him, that He can inspire our hearts and thoughts toward the best solution. The final result must always be something that will bring glory and honor to God. The Bible tells us that the Holy Spirit will lead us into all truth. However, He must do the leading. A chain or a rope can't be pushed. It must be led or pulled. The chain or rope does not determine where it will go or what it will do. Someone else makes those decisions, and so it is with us.

God's checking account is never overdrawn. He is never in a quandary about how to solve a dilemma. He still owns the cattle on a thousand hills. All of earth's resources still belong to Him. He's not broke, and He's never confused. Furthermore, God says that He will take the wealth of the wicked and give it to His children. He has more ingenious ways than we can ever dare to imagine, to bring a happy solution to our problems.

Trust in the LORD with all thine heart;
and lean not unto thine own
understanding. In all thy ways

---

acknowledge him, and he shall direct thy paths. Proverbs 3:5-6

But they that wait upon the LORD shall renew their strength; they shall mount up with wings as eagles; they shall run, and not be weary; and they shall walk, and not faint. Isaiah 40:31

This is another great song of faith that we sang at the cemetery following my son's funeral on October 17, 1995:

> ## I WILL CAST ALL MY CARES
> *Liz Ashwoon, copyright 1994,*
> *Out of the Door Music*
>
> I will cast all my cares upon You, Lord.
> I will lay all of my burdens down at your feet.
> And anytime I don't know just what to do
> I will cast all my care upon Him.

DON'T PLAY GAMES WITH GOD

So many times, when we hit a tough spot, we try to bribe God to do something special on our behalf. In return, we make wild promises to God that everyone knows we can't keep. Our negotiating technique may sound something like this: "Oh, God, if only you will do this for me, I promise that I will..." or perhaps it might sound a bit more like this, "God, if I could pay my bills, then I would be glad to tithe." Or, "If I could get a raise from my boss, I would be glad to work harder," or "If only I felt better, then I could praise the Lord." Another rendition could also be "If only I had a friend, then I could be one."

In all of these situations, note that the cart is in front of the horse. We cannot expect to pick beans from our garden if we have planted corn. We plant or sow seeds, and later on reap abundantly the same things we sowed. God's laws of nature are very specific about this. The only way we can expect to receive something in return is *after* we plant the seed, not *before*. Therefore, we aren't going to get very far with God by trying to con Him into doing something for us first, on the promise that we will follow through afterwards. He knows our hearts. He knows what is really going on inside. It still comes back to a matter of our faith in God's promises and our obedience to what His Word has already instructed us to do. Only then do we have the right to expect the desired outcome to occur.

> *And he gave them their request; but sent leanness into their soul. Psalms 106:15*

This Scripture always sobers me. It refers to the experience of the children of Israel as they traveled through the wilderness on their way to the Promised Land. Instead of being grateful for the many things God was providing for them, they began to think about the things they had left behind in Egypt. They began murmuring and complaining, activities that always make God angry. He responded to their griping by giving them the things they demanded, but the result was a serious deficiency in their spiritual relationship with Him. Yes, they did bargain and receive what they wanted from God, but things didn't turn out at all like they thought they would. They seriously regretted getting the things they asked God to provide.

Is there anything or anyone in your life that you think you can't live without? Is anything causing you to complain and gripe? I urgently caution you to reevaluate this attitude, because God just might give you your demands, and forever you will seriously regret thinking you couldn't live without that person or thing. God is most interested in having an intimate personal relationship with you. He must become your highest priority. Anything that breaks your fellowship with God is serious business.

There is another old hymn that I love to sing. It goes like this:

GOD LEADS US ALONG
G. A. Young, (public domain)

In shady, green pastures, so rich and so sweet,
God leads His dear children along;
Where the water's cold flow bathes the weary one's feet,
God leads His dear children along.

Sometimes on the mount where the sun shines so bright,
God leads His dear children along;
Sometimes in the valley, in darkest of night,
God leads His dear children along.

Though sorrows befall us, and Satan

oppose,
God leads His dear children along;
Through grace we can conquer, defeat all
our foes,
God leads His dear children along.

Away from the mire, and away from the
clay,
God leads His dear children along;
Away up in glory, eternity's day,
God leads His dear children along.

Chorus—
Some through the waters, some through the
flood,
Some through the fire, but all through the
blood;
Some through great sorrow, but God gives a
song,
In the night-season and all the day long.

DON'T FRET AND WORRY

Doubting, fretting and worrying are very normal, human activities to be involved in. Some of us are a whole lot better at doing them than others are, because we have never come to point where we properly discipline our minds. This can only be accomplished by submitting ourselves to the Holy Spirit and to the Word of God. Faith and fear cannot co-exist in our hearts and minds. One or the other always has the upper hand, depending on which one we cater to. Thus, we contribute to either the problem or the solution by our own decision. Fretting and worrying are just expressions of doubt, lack of faith or uncertainty that God is really able to keep His promises and effectively deal with the problems. We quickly forget that, if God has promised in His Word that He will do something, He is fully able to do it. He doesn't lie. He doesn't mislead His people. We need to better learn how to stand on His promises and let God be God.

For the weapons of our warfare are not carnal, but mighty through God to the pulling down of strong holds; casting down imaginations, and every high thing that exalteth itself against the knowledge of God, and bringing into captivity every thought to the obedience of Christ..." II Corinthians 10:4-5

Cease from anger, and forsake wrath: fret not thyself in any wise to do evil. Psalm 37:8

Now faith is the substance of things hoped for, the evidence of things not seen. Hebrews 11:1

Fear not: for I have redeemed thee, I have called thee by thy name; thou art mine. When thou passest through the waters, I will be with thee; and through the rivers, they shall not overflow thee: when thou walkest through the fire, thou shalt not be burned; neither shall the flame kindle upon thee. Isaiah 43:1-2

CHAPTER SIX

A book written by Dr. Robert Schuller, of the "Hour of Power" television program, is entitled: Tough Times Don't Last, But Tough People Do. I enjoyed reading the book and felt that I could identify with his thoughts. The Scriptures do *not* indicate that Christians will be free from problems in this life, but they do say that we *will survive* and overcome them. The Scripture I just quoted from Isaiah 43 uses the word "through" instead of "into." As Christians, we may go *through* the water and the fire in this life, but we won't stay there forever. We are going to come out victoriously on the other side. God is not going to abandon us in the middle of a conflict or problem. He will be with us to help us overcome and be victorious. God will make sure of it. One of my favorite verses in the Bible is one that is repeated many times throughout the New Testament, "...and it came to pass." Many events take place in our lives. They don't come to stay; they come to *pass*. It won't always be like it is right now. Give it time, and your situation will change. God is in control, and things will get better. God won't forget about you and your desperate need.

DON'T BECOME BITTER

There are many things that happen to us that simply are not right. They are not fair and should never happen. Someone takes advantage of us, cheats us, or robs us of something very special. These are very difficult situations to deal with, even for those who think of themselves as quite spiritual and close to God. Even if we do not deserve the terrible treatment we receive, we must never allow a root of bitterness to germinate in our hearts. If we do, bitterness will quickly blossom and eventually destroy us, one way or another. We will be the one who is affected the most by our bitterness, and we will find ourselves quickly debilitated. The person who caused the pain in the first place, the one we might feel deserves to be damaged, just goes on with life as though nothing happened. Bitterness is like a cancer. It only gets worse with time. Therefore, we must deal it with quickly and properly. The hurt feelings, the injustice, the rage, and the anger must be nipped in the bud and not allowed to remain in our hearts. Those who hurt us and did damage to us will likely be completely oblivious to the sorrow and pain they caused us. That is why carrying a grudge against someone is a luxury that none of us can afford. The Bible is very clear that we cannot expect the Lord to forgive us *our* misdeeds if we *cannot* forgive, or we *refuse* to forgive, other people their misdeeds. This is very serious business, because we totally block the ability of the Lord to forgive us. Therefore, the only person who ultimately loses the most after a bout with bitterness is the person who hangs unto bitterness.

Vengeance is mine. I will repay, saith the Lord. Romans 12:19

Cease from anger, and forsake wrath; fret not thyself in any wise to do evil. Psalm 37:8

And forgive us our debts, as we forgive our debtors...For if ye forgive men their trespasses, your heavenly Father will also forgive you: But if ye forgive not men their

> *trespasses, neither will your Father*
> *forgive your trespasses. Matthew :12-15*

This is pretty serious business when we realize that we can actually block God's ability to forgive us by the attitude we display towards those who hurt us. Our faith, as well as our testimony for the Lord, will eventually be totally destroyed. Though we may feel the offender does not deserve to be forgiven, we must never forget that we don't deserve to be forgiven either. No one deserves to be forgiven. Even if the offender has not asked for forgiveness, we must still forgive him. This is the example set for us by our Lord. We must let the Lord take care of that person, while we focus upon ways to let the love of Christ flow through us to that person. God knows what happened, and He will take care of it. He will rectify things in His time.

> *And when ye stand praying, forgive, if ye have ought against any: that your Father also which is in Heaven may forgive you your trespasses. Mark 11:25*
>
> *... and forgiving one another, if any man have a quarrel against any: even as Christ forgave you, so also do ye. Colossians 3:13*
>
> *Looking diligently lest any man fail of the grace of God; lest any root of bitterness springing up trouble you, and thereby many be defiled; Hebrews 12:15*
>
> *For all the law is fulfilled in one word, even in this: THOU SHALT LOVE THY*

*NEIGHBOR AS THYSELF. But if ye bite
and devour one another, take heed that ye
not be consumed one by another.*
Galatians 5:14-15

I think that this prayer chorus is very fitting at this point:

LET THE BEAUTY OF JESUS
*Tom Jones/Albert Osborn/George L.
Johnson, (public domain)*

Let the beauty of Jesus be seen in me,
All His wonderful passion and purity.
Oh, thou Spirit Divine, all my nature refine,
Till the beauty of Jesus be seen in me.

DON'T MURMUR OR COMPLAIN

Whatever happened has already happened. Painful experiences are difficult to accept, because we spend so much time thinking about the things that might have been. We may even wish that we could go back and relive some of our experiences, because we know we would react or respond differently, now that we see things in a different perspective. It is very likely that nothing will ever be completely the same in your life again. None of us can return to the way things were once upon a time, to the "good old days." Therefore, we must move on with life, letting the past be past, and trusting God that there will indeed be better days ahead. If we sit around wallowing in a massive pity party, we focus upon all of the things that

HOW TO KEEP YOUR FAITH **167**

are wrong, the things we don't like, and the things we wish we could change. Thus, we simply short-circuit God's plan. We hamstring His ability to minister to us and use us to be a blessing to others. God did not allow this circumstance, problem or difficulty to come into our life to frustrate, condemn, or confuse us. He wants us to know that we can rise above whatever it is, and find out, first hand, that God is *really* for real. This is our big chance to find out that God's promises in the Bible really *do* apply to us, that they are *still* appropriate for us today. We have a tendency to get very comfortable and secure, as long as everything is going just right in our lives. However, God wants to get us out of our comfort zone, to grow and mature spiritually, so that He can demonstrate His power and love in our lives. When unexpected events occur in our lives, our attitude and response is most critical. If all we want to do is to grumble and gripe, we will never experience the joy and victory that God wants us to know.

> *I said, I will take heed of my ways, that I sin not with my tongue; I will keep my mouth with a bridle while the wicked is before me. Psalms 39:1*

We must always remember that the ungodly are watching the people of God, to note how they react to the circumstances of life. If we end up responding exactly the same way they would, they will never have any recognition of their need for a Savior. They will see no benefit to making a change in their lives.

DON'T CARRY THE BURDEN ALONE

There is definite merit in just fervently praying privately about our personal needs and the problems that occur in our lives. However, God, in His infinite wisdom, designed all Christian believers with a purpose of functioning actively in His Body, the Church. The Church is a living organism, divinely planned to function on earth and carry out His plans and purposes with the help of the Holy Spirit. If our spiritual brothers and sisters, fellow members of that Church, are not even aware that we are experiencing a need or a problem, there is no way they can effectively minister to us or assist us. None of us was designed by God to be a super hero, one that does not require the love and support from the Body of Christ. From the least to the greatest, we all need each other desperately. The Body of Christ contains many members, each with different functions. It remains healthy and productive as each part of the Body performs its duties properly. That means that both giving and receiving must occur regularly for every member. Each individual member is extremely vital to the well-being of the others. The Bible tells us in James chapter five, that we are to confess our weaknesses and faults to each other. The purpose of this is so we can pray more effectively for each other. We are to love each other, just as we love Christ and He loves us. If some parts of the Body of Christ crawl off by themselves into a hole, because of problems and difficulties going on in their lives, how can the body be expected to function properly? Every part of the Body must remain in its position and function as it was designed.

Blessed be God, even the Father of our Lord Jesus Christ, the Father of mercies, and the God of all comfort; who comforteth us in all our tribulation, that we may be able to comfort them which are in any trouble, by the comfort wherewith we ourselves are comforted of God. II Corinthians 1:3-4

By this shall all men know that ye are my disciples, if ye have love one to another. John 13:35

And whether one member suffers, all the members suffer with it; or one member be honoured, all the members rejoice with it. Now ye are the body of Christ, and members in particular. 1 Corinthians 12:26-27

WE WILL STAND
Russ Taff/ Tori Taff/ James Hollihan
copyright 1983 Word Music, Inc.

You're my brother, You're my sister,
So take me by the hand.
Together we will work until He comes.
There's no foe that can defeat us,
We're walking side by side.
As long as there is love
We will stand.

DON'T FOCUS UPON ANOTHER TIME

Today is the first day of the rest of our lives. Today is the day that the Lord has made. Let us rejoice and be glad in it. Today is a very important day for us, because it is the only day that we can do anything about. The past has already occurred. There is absolutely nothing that we can do to ever change what has already happened. Tomorrow is not here yet, and may not even come for some of us. The only way that we can change anything about tomorrow, is to change what we are doing or thinking today. We cannot live in the past. Neither can we live in the future yet. We can only enjoy living *this* day to the fullest possible measure, the day that we have been given.

When God provided the special miracle food, manna, during the journey of the children of Israel from Egypt to the Promised Land, He provided just enough of it for one day at a time. The only exception to this rule was the two-day's supply on Fridays, so they wouldn't have to collect any on the Sabbath, the day of rest. If someone tried to collect a two-day's supply on any other day, it got worms in it. Likely no one tried that more than once, but in any crowd, there are usually people who don't follow instructions very well or who try to cut corners. The children of Israel found out very quickly that God meant business, that His commands were not just suggestions. When He told them that He would take care of them on a daily basis, He meant it.

If we try to live in the past, rehashing all of the blessings or pains of yesterday, we will likely find "worms" in our manna too. God wants us to focus upon today. God has promised to meet our needs for today. For some strange reason, some of God's children prefer to think about tomorrow most of the time. They love to spend a significant portion of their time thinking about heaven and all of the future blessings promised to the children of God. They forget to focus upon doing anything worthwhile today. Their favorite song seems to be, "Won't It Be Wonderful *There*?" Other children of God are hung up on all of the blessings of yesterday, the way it used to be. Their favorite song is, "Wasn't It Wonderful *Then*." It has been said that some people are so heavenly-minded that they are of no earthly good. Others are so earthly-minded that they are no heavenly good. We need to keep a good balance in our lives, between the past and the future, so that we can be effective in making a difference in the lives of others today.

> *Take therefore no thought for the morrow: for the morrow shall take thought for the things of itself. Sufficient unto the day is the evil thereof. Matthew 6:34*

A praise chorus taken from Scripture goes like this:

THIS IS THE DAY
Les Garrett, copyright 1967, 1980, Scripture in Song

This is the day. This is the day
That the Lord hath made - that the Lord hath made.
I will rejoice, I will rejoice

And be glad in it. And be glad in it
This is the day that that the Lord hath made.
I will rejoice and be glad in it.
This is the day, this is the day that the Lord
hath made.

DON'T LOSE YOUR SENSE OF HUMOR

I know, from personal experience, that it is not always easy to smile though your tears or to really "laugh in the Spirit," as the Bible tells us. However, Christian believers must understand the total futility of the enemy's efforts to defeat or destroy us. There is a genuine benefit available for us who rise above the pain and the distress of the moment, who keep a positive attitude about things, by looking for the humor in something that has happened, even something painful. I didn't say it was easy, but I can assure you that there is a lot of humor in many things that happen, provided you see them in the proper light. Those who have no connection with the power of God haven't this ability within themselves, but God *does* have a great sense of humor. How He just "happens" to bring people together at just the right moment, or how He just "happens" to work out intricate timing so that a need is met just in the nick of time, never ceases to amaze me. He really is a great God, and His love for us is beyond measure and human understanding. That is why it is so desperately important for us not to get "down in the dumps" on God.

*A merry heart doeth good like a
medicine...Proverbs 17:22*

All the days of the afflicted are evil, but he that is of a merry heart hath a continual feast. Proverbs 15:15

Wherein ye greatly rejoice, though now for a season, if need be, ye are in heaviness through manifold temptations: That the trial of your faith, being much more precious than of gold that perisheth, though it be tried with fire, might be found unto praise and honour and glory at the appearing of Jesus Christ: 1 Peter 1:6-7

My brethren, count it all joy when ye fall into divers temptations, knowing this: that the trying of your faith worketh patience.But let patience have her perfect work, that ye may be perfect and entire, lacking nothing. James 1:2-4

Rejoice in the Lord always: and again I say, Rejoice. Philippians 4:4

These Scriptures are not talking about rejoicing and being happy just when we feel cheerful or humorous. They are speaking about an attitude, a step of faith, even a lifestyle, knowing that God always has everything under control. Whatever He eventually works out in our lives will be something good, something great, something worth experiencing. We can count on it. Knowing this helps us relax and step back, so that God can help us see the big picture. By faith, we begin anticipating the future blessings He will bring about in our lives to replace the present pain and sorrow.

I have long loved this little chorus.

I AM BLESSED
Mike Murdock

When I think about my fam'ly
and the love that I've received,
And all my friends God has given to me;
And I look all around me at the God things
that I see,
I am blessed. I am blessed!

When I recall the miles I've traveled east to
west,
His grace has been sufficient to pass ev'ry
test;
And the health God has given me has been
the very best,
I am blessed. I am blessed!

I am blessed. I am blessed.
Every day that I live, I am blessed;
When I wake up in the morning
or I lay my head to rest,
I am blessed. I am blessed!

DON'T LOOK TO THE 'ARM OF FLESH'

It is highly probable, that in bringing about the needed
answer or solution in our lives, God will use other people
to minister healing or deliverance to us, people anointed
by the power of the Holy Spirit. That is a very typical way

for God to operate. However, it is very important for us to realize that it is not up to us to choose whom He may use for that task. God is perfectly capable of choosing the right person to help us, or to give us a specific word from Him. We still need to keep our focus off people and upon the Lord. He is still the one true source of whatever we need. If your experience has been similar to mine, you will agree that it is *people,* not the *Lord,* who have let us down. *They* have been the ones who disappointed us, or who came against us. This is the primary reason that our "giving of alms" to those in need must follow the pattern shown in Scripture. It must be done "in secret," not openly. Otherwise, a needy person with a new crisis in the future, will likely simply bypass praying to God about it, and go directly to the person who met the need the last time. God might want to use someone *else* next time there is a need, not the same person. God is still sovereign and must stay in complete control of every dilemma, so He can work out all of the intricate details of meeting our need.

Furthermore, I have found that there is no end to the scope of personal opinions people have about every possible subject. If we always consult with other people, rather than the Lord, we will become extremely confused. Their opinion may not necessarily be the voice of the Holy Spirit that God has sent to "lead us into all truth." When the chips are down and we really need a miracle, we need the Holy Spirit to supernaturally direct us to the person who will have a message from the Lord. However, God's messages to us are already very clear in His Word, and we usually don't need to have any further instruction. We just need to obey what we already know the Bible tell us to do.

It is amazing how many of God's children spend major time and money running all over the country during a crisis, looking desperately for a healer, a prophet, or a wizard of some kind to minister the power of God to them. I don't sit in criticism of them, but I wonder why God can't use someone local who can accomplish this just as effectively. The prayer of faith does not need to be prayed over us by a nationally-known evangelist, a pastor, or the author of a newly published book. God may just want to use that person sitting there beside you right now, to pray the prayer of faith over you.

Behold, I am the LORD, the God of all flesh: is there anything too hard for me? Jeremiah 32:27

The steps of a good man are ordered by the Lord; and he delighteth in his way. Though he fall, he shall not be utterly cast down; for the Lord upholdeth him with his hand. Psalm 37:23

Thou art the God that doest wonders: thou hast declared thy strength among the people. Psalm 77:14

I really like the meaning of this beautiful chorus:

IN HIS TIME
Diane Ball, copyright 1978
Maranatha! Music

In His time, in His time;

He makes all things beautiful in His time.
Lord, please show me every day, as You're
teaching me Your way,
That you do just what you say in your time.

In Your time, in Your time;
You make all things beautiful in Your time.
Lord, my life to You I bring
May each song I have to sing
Be to a You a lovely thing
In Your time.

DON'T HAVE A 'GRASSHOPPER COMPLEX'

There is another very interesting episode about the children of Israel, recorded in the Old Testament in Numbers chapters 13 and 14. After traveling for a time in the wilderness, from Egypt, they approached the border of Canaan. Moses decided to send twelve spies, one from each tribe, to see what The Promised Land was like. Everyone in the nation of Israel was very curious to know more about their new homeland, and they anxiously awaited the return of the spies with their report. When they did return, they brought back exciting news about the marvelous things awaiting them. They even brought back samples of the lush fruit. The country was everything God had promised it would be, but there was one major hitch. They found many super giants there. Ten of the spies expressed great concern over this. The other two spies, Joshua and Caleb, responded that God, who had brought them this far on their journey, was fully able to help them defeat the giants. In spite of this message of faith, paranoia spread rapidly among the people. Numbers 13:33 says that they felt like grasshoppers before the giants. All twelve of the spies had seen the same things. They all brought back an accurate report. The children of Israel were ready to break camp and start moving into Canaan, until they listened to the majority of the spies and became filled with fear.

Fear is a strange thing. It can cause reason and faith to vanish. It can make any task or challenge seem totally impossible. If, when you face an opportunity or challenge, you see yourself as a grasshopper, in comparison to the major problem or challenge, you will determine that you are whipped before you start. With that attitude, you will not succeed in any endeavor. It won't matter anymore what God has promised. You're doomed to experience defeat in everything you attempt. Faith and fear cannot co-exist. The very interesting thing about all of this, is that the way you see things is absolute reality for you. Everyone sees things through either the eye of faith or the eye of fear. The choice is yours, but the two cannot co-exist.

The children of Israel began to wish they were still in slavery back in Egypt. They forgot all of the miracles that God had already performed to bring them this far. Murmuring and complaining spread like wildfire throughout the camp. The ten spies who were overcome with a bad case of "low self-esteem," were able to destroy the impact of the good report Joshua and Caleb brought. As a result, God said that none of them, except Joshua and Caleb, would ever get to see the Promised Land. They would all die in the wilderness before they arrived. If they preferred to believe that God was not able to help them defeat the enemies dwelling in the land God had promised to give them, God would allow them to experience exactly what they had the faith or the fear to believe for. The things they confessed with their mouths ended up limiting God from fulfilling His promises to them. God was still able to do what He had promised, but their fear overpowered God's ability to perform. Only those who were under the age of twenty would ever get to experience what God had in mind for them in Canaan. They lost out on what God wanted to give them, because they allowed a "grasshopper complex" to paralyze them and destroy their ability to believe the promises God had given them.

Therefore, it is very important to take note of *how* we see something. How we see something depends a great deal upon how we see ourselves. This will take into account our strengths and our weaknesses, as well as how we approach life in general. We have a tendency to see either the possibilities or the problems. We see either the opportunities or potential disaster. We see either success or a major failure. It is true that our vantage provides us with a very realistic perspective. We are dealing with factual data, but we might not be seeing the full picture. What we are viewing might be distorted because of the way that we see ourselves, as well as how we see God. What we are seeing might appear to be much bigger than we are, even impossible to overcome, but it is at a time like this that we have an important choice to make. We can focus upon the problem or we can focus upon the solution.

Joshua and Caleb came back to the camp with a different report. They chose to see the situation through the eyes of faith, rather than through the eyes of doubt and fear. They chose to remember that God had already kept His promises to deliver them this far on their journey. They wanted nothing to do with the suggestion of going back into slavery in Egypt. Their eyes were on how great the Promised Land was, and how good it was going to be living there. It is important to remember the majority is not *always* right. All ten of the spies had a choice to make, and they chose to see what they wanted to.

I love this precious song that we often sing.

BECAUSE HE LIVES
Willilam J. Gaither, copyright 1971
William J. Gaither, Inc.

God sent His son, they called Him Jesus.
He came to love, heal and forgive.
He lived and died to buy my pardon.
An empty grave is there to prove my Savior lives.

And then one day I'll cross the river.
I'll fight life's final war with pain.
And then as death gives way to victory,
I'll see the lights of glory, and I'll know He lives.

Chorus—
Because He lives, I can face tomorrow.
Because He lives, all fear is gone.
Because I know, I know He holds the future,

| And life is worth the living, just because He lives. |

DON'T BLAME OTHERS

It is very normal to try to make ourselves look better in someone else's eyes, as well as our own. We enjoy having an opportunity to "pass the buck" of fault or failure onto someone else's back, so we don't have to take responsibility for the part we played in creating a mess. There are many people who go through their entire lives refusing to admit that they are ever in the wrong. Apologizing or asking someone else to forgive them is not part of their vocabulary. They feverishly blame everything bad on other people. This actually becomes a lifestyle that is extremely difficult to change, but it must change before worthwhile improvements can ever be made in our personal circumstances.

Sometimes the roots of this character trait go back to our childhood, when our parents or someone else planted the idea in our minds that we could do nothing wrong. As we grew up, we found that if we could put the blame for a problem on someone else, we could escape most, if not all, of the consequences of our actions. There are many people in jails and prisons of our country, who still struggle with taking the blame for their wrong conduct. There are many others who will never make a good marriage mate, employee, or neighbor, because they always skillfully avoid taking personal responsibility for their lousy behavior or actions. They vehemently declare their innocence, and sincerely believe that all of their problems are entirely the result of someone else's mistakes, not their own.

I have observed that individuals who insist on maintaining this perspective of life are never able to really get a grip on life and achieve measurable success levels. They spend so much time and effort whining and complaining about how unfairly they are being treated, that they are never able to make any significant progress toward a sense of fulfillment and achievement. They always see themselves as victims of circumstances, and they will never be in the "driver's seat" of their lives. God expects all of us to take control of our lives and to be fully accountable for our own conduct and attitude. Until we achieve that necessary control, we will just spend our time and effort feeling sorry for ourselves, and we will always feel defeated and out of step with the rest of the world.

Admit mistakes. Take responsibility for errors made. When that occurs, God will respond positively and begin providing the ability and strength to change the particular set of circumstances plaguing us. He will help us see ourselves as overcomers and victors through Christ, which is much more appropriate than seeing ourselves as helpless victims.

HEALING AND RESTORATION

THE FIRST DAY OF THE REST OF MY LIFE

When I was growing up, I frequently heard a comment that went like this, "Vell, I yust can't vin for loosing," which is interpreted from the Scandinavian accent to mean, "Well, I just can't win for losing." At first hearing, this sounds like an innocent statement for making conversation or passing time, but I am personally convinced that people who make comments like that are not aware of what they are *really* saying. Perhaps their comments are nothing more than a casual statement or expression that was copied and passed down, from generation to generation, going back to the time of the Mayflower coming to America. Regardless, the Bible makes it clear that whatever comes out of our mouths is a reflection of what is in our hearts.

As a man thinketh in his heart, so is he.
Proverbs 23:7

Whoso keepeth his mouth and his tongue keeping his soul from troubles. Proverbs 21:23

Death and life are in the power of the tongue...Proverbs 18:21

Our conversation reveals everything about our secret thoughts and basic attitudes. When we speak of ourselves as being losers, we are actually declaring that everything that happens to us is unfair, negative or working against us. Our self-image has taken a major beating because of the events of life, and we are expressing the feeling that there is absolutely nothing we can do to change anything. We are helpless, hopeless victims of circumstances beyond our control, and thus, we have no personal responsibility to change our thinking or our attitude. I firmly *disagree* with this logic or philosophy of life. We not only *can* change our thinking and attitude, but we *must*. What we repeatedly speak with our lips is what we eventually act out and ultimately become, because "out of the abundance of the heart, the mouth speaketh." (Matthew 12:34) What we say about ourselves becomes a self-fulfilling prophecy, whether it is a positive statement or a negative one. We automatically believe the things we say about ourselves, and our actions soon follow our beliefs. We determine our own outcome by the things we declare about ourselves from our hearts via our mouths. Therefore, before we can change or modify our circumstances, we have to change or modify what we are thinking and feeling about ourselves, deep inside our hearts. Then, and only then, will we see a change in the external circumstances.

In a similar vein, I came across a statement credited to Charles Swindoll, a well-known pastor heard on our local Christian radio station. He said, "The longer I live, the more convinced I am that having a winning attitude in life is not affected as much by what *happens* to me, as it is by how I *react* to what happens to me." I strongly agree. I emphatically declare myself to be *a winner, not a loser.* When bad or negative things happen to me, I am convinced I will overcome and win, regardless of what I am experiencing. To illustrate this conviction, I made a little sign for the credenza behind the desk at my office, which declares, "I can't lose for winning." I know what the Word of God says about me, and I know that God still has everything perfectly under control. I also know that, in spite of trouble and severe loss, I *will* survive and be victorious. I *shall* prevail, because the Bible says I am more than a conqueror through Christ Jesus who loves me. (Romans 8:37) It also tells me that I am a child of the King, a joint-heir with Jesus, a man after God's own heart, a servant unto righteousness. I know where I'm going, and I know Who is going with me. I *can't* lose for very long, though I still occasionally suffer loss.

It is very important that we Christian believers see ourselves as God sees us, because we are the handiwork of His creation. We are not our own. We have been bought with a great price. We are His precious treasure. He gave up *everything* for us. Thus, we are very important to God. We must never allow ourselves to look like "an accident going somewhere to happen," or act like "a tin can on a dog's tail." Our circumstances are not to master us. We are to master them. There are no real accidents for us as children of God, because everything that happens to us is part of His perfect plan. Nothing that happens to us catches God by surprise. Whatever our enemy intends for evil, God simply turns into something for our good, even if it takes awhile for it to happen. We can count on it. Knowing this important fact really takes the stress and uncertainty out of life.

To illustrate this, let's consider the major differences between a thermometer and a thermostat. A thermometer simply tells it like it is, by accurately reporting the temperature. It is factual and usually quite dependable. It doesn't lie. However, a thermometer can't *do anything* about the temperature. It just reports it. A thermostat is very different. It accurately reports the room temperature, but it also modifies it to a desired setting. Furthermore, once the desired temperature is reached, a thermostat maintains it. Similarly, people respond to life situations like either thermometers or thermostats. We should prefer to be more like thermostats. We have the God-given ability to change things. We are able to *change* our minds and attitudes. Therefore we can impact our environment and our circumstances, and have better control over the outcome.

GET RID OF EXCESS BAGGAGE

One of the many exciting things I did several years ago was take flying lessons. There is no way to fully describe the thrill I experienced at the controls of even a simple plane like a Cessna 150. After every thrilling takeoff, I was able to climb high and float above all of the problems that I left behind on earth. I will never forget the experience of flying a required "solo cross-country" trip. I decided to fly from Sioux Falls, to Pierre, to Rapid City, and then home again. I have had lots of wonderful experiences in life, but few can match this one. After having received extensive joint-flying experience with my instructor, I was now authorized to apply my newly-acquired skills in the pilot's seat by flying alone on a lengthy, cross-country trip, making landings in three different airports. It was awesome having to rapidly recall the many rules and regulations that a pilot must follow in order to adjust for air traffic, weather conditions, and takeoff/landing procedures in controlled or uncontrolled airports (with or without control towers). I remember watching my gas gauge very carefully as I got closer to the home-base airport on the return leg. When the plane was refueled after my landing, I was informed that I had landed with only two gallons in the tank. I was very fortunate that I didn't have a literal "let-down-experience" on my hands.

As a pilot, one of the basic elements I needed to learn about flying an airplane, was that drag could not exceed lift. No airplane gets off the runway if its weight surpasses its horsepower. This simple formula must be applied to our personal lives as well. If we are trying to carry "too much baggage," we will never get anywhere, either in life or in the air. We can make a lot of impressive noise. We can appear to have great possibilities. We can have all of the necessary qualifications. We can look like we are serious and really mean business, but we will never get off the ground, at least for very long, if we are "over-loaded." We have to eliminate whatever baggage weighs us down and holds us back from our potential achievements. That is a price we must be willing to pay, in order to experience the euphoria of flying "above the clouds, above the storms of life," just like an eagle.

Another important lesson I learned about life while taking flying lessons was that I needed faith in my instruments, and I had to know how to read an aeronautical map. That was especially true when flying in inclement weather. I dared not trust my basic instincts of direction or position. I had to learn to watch my instruments and be willing to obey verbal instructions from the authority in the tower. This was definitely not the time to try to fly "by the seat of my pants." I had to fly by a different set of rules under these conditions. They are called IFR, or instrument flight rules, rather than VFR, visual flight rules. I didn't have time to start reading the rulebook when I got into bad weather. I needed to know the rules ahead of time, so I could automatically do the right thing at the right time. That required some advance effort and attention on my part. Furthermore, all of this demanded a certain amount of faith. I needed to have faith in the person(s) who wrote the rulebook and drew the maps, faith in the one who created and installed the instruments I saw in front of me, as well as faith in the one whose voice I heard giving me specific directions from the tower. In order to be a successful pilot, I needed to discipline myself to know and follow the rules of flying, or my future was truly in major jeopardy.

It seems there are many spiritual applications for life in this illustration as well. It is imperative that we be willing to trust the Word of God to provide the necessary instructions for life. We dare not wait until we get into a storm before we start studying and memorizing His Word. In times of crisis, we need to be able to respond automatically and follow the correct procedures immediately. We have to fully trust the sovereign God who wrote that precious book, over a period of many years, by anointing certain people with His Holy Spirit. He is the same God who created and knew us, even the day when we would be born and the day when we would die, from the beginning of time. Furthermore, we have to respond quickly in obedience when His Holy Spirit speaks to our hearts with specific instructions, so He can direct us around, over, under, or through the storms of life, and lead us safely home to heaven. As in following the rules of flying, we need to discipline ourselves to know and follow God's rules, or our eternal future is in jeopardy.

KEEP YOUR EYE ON A WORTHY GOAL

Another experience that provides a significant spiritual lesson, relates to a task I performed as a kid, growing up on a farm in South Dakota. I was often recruited to do the plowing. This job became one of my favorites, though it certainly was a monotonous one. It required that I take the tractor with the attached plow out to the field. There I dropped the plow into the ground at one end of the field, and drove to the opposite end of the field, keeping one tractor tire in the furrow left from the previous round. I would lift the plow, turn the tractor around, and follow the return furrow back to where I had started. This process was repeated round after round, until I finally got the entire field plowed. That really wasn't a terribly difficult assignment. Moreover, it provided an extraordinary opportunity for some important daydreaming about what I might want to do with my life, something more exciting than plowing. It was a great time for singing and praying. I could also observe what was going on in the sky or in my neighbor's field, and I could make great plans for the weekend.

Though plowing was a bit dull and tedious, it also afforded some unique challenges. One of these occurred whenever I "laid out a new land." When I finished plowing the section of ground I was working on, I needed to move further down the field to start the first furrow in a new section of the field. Since there was no old furrow to follow, I needed to carefully determine where I wanted to begin and where I wanted to go, in order to get to the other side of the field with my initial furrow. If I did it right, the new furrow would be straight and easy to follow. Then I could continue round after round, until I eventually completed plowing this new section of the field. The real secret to creating a straight initial furrow was to fix my eyes upon a proper goal at the other end of the field. I dared not allow any distractions to take my eyes off that goal until I arrived at the other end of the field. Hopefully, I wouldn't hit an underground rock that would cause the plow to disengage from the tractor. If that happened, I would have to stop and back up to reattach the plow. All of this activity would seriously affect my straight furrow.

The very worst thing to do, however, was to wonder whether or not I was plowing a straight furrow, and be tempted to turn around in the seat to check my progress. If I yielded to that temptation, the very act of turning around in my seat would cause me to slightly turn the steering wheel. The result would be a slight crook in the furrow. The second worst thing that I could do was to select a goal that would move before I got to the other side of the field. This movable goal could be a cow or a neighbor on his tractor. In spite of good intentions, I occasionally goofed. I remember several times when I had to work quickly to try to straighten out a crooked furrow. I didn't want my dad, or someone else driving by, to wonder what in the world I had been thinking about to cause me to screw up such a simple task.

There are two very important lessons or principles of life that I gleaned from this regular experience on the farm. The first one was that I always needed to keep my eyes fixed upon a worthy goal, and not allow anything else to distract me until I got my job done. I was reminded of the Scripture verse in Luke 9:62 which declares, " No one having put his hand to the plow, and looking back, is fit for the Kingdom of God." The second important principle was that even if I *did* make an occasional goof-up, I just needed to keep working diligently, and not quit or worry needlessly about making a mistake. None of my plowing mistakes would ever show up once the entire field was plowed, except to someone who was just looking for mistakes. All of the crooked furrows would be obliterated then. Therefore, I must not quit my task just because I made a mistake while plowing, just as I must not give up if I make mistakes in other areas of life. I needed to stay focused upon my assignment and keep being productive. Eventually, the mistakes would be forgotten or set aside, because they would be obliterated in the scope of a greater accomplishment. Even the future harvest will not be impacted greatly by some mistakes I made in my plowing. Likewise, the Lord can still use me effectively, though I still make mistakes, as long as I don't sit down and quit. Continued productivity will eventually diminish the effects of a crooked furrow, as well as other mistakes that are made in life.

I must admit that the multiple struggles and problems I have encountered have severely shaken me, but they have been unable to shake my faith in a *good God*. As I am experiencing the things that only God can do in my life, my faith in Him is simply growing stronger. Instead of dislodging me, the storms of life have forced my roots to grow deeper into the strength and nourishment that God provides for His children. I continue standing in awe of the mighty ways He demonstrates His power and love to me. I still occasionally have a bad day, but there are a whole lot more good ones. God alone enables me to survive my traumatic experiences and live a victorious life.

I am particularly encouraged when someone tells me they are praying for me. I know, from experience, how important that knowledge is. Therefore, God has inspired me to pray more faithfully for other people during their times of trial, and to inform them I am praying. None of us is an "island unto ourselves." There is great value in God's people sticking together through tough times. The awareness that someone else is "standing in the gap" for us provides a tremendous source of strength and encouragement. We're not abandoned and left all alone in the midst of the struggle.

There is also a scriptural law for us to consider. That law is the law of sowing and reaping, of seedtime and harvest. The very same things that we desperately need in our lives, may be the same things we need to sow, or give, into the lives of others. For instance, if I find myself pressed for more time, I may need to give more of my time away. If I find myself needing more love or attention, I may need to give more love to others. If I am experiencing a financial shortfall, I may need to sow or give away more of my finances. If I feel that no one appreciates me, I may need to be more appreciative of others. I can't realistically expect God to provide the things I need in my life, unless I have first been faithful in my sowing. There will be no reaping without sowing first. Seed in the bag can never produce a return. There is no such thing as a spiritual volunteer crop that just grows automatically without a seed being planted. The only things that grow profusely without being planted are weeds. I must sow the things I eventually expect to receive. The things sown produce a crop of the same kind. I will *not* reap the things I have *not* sown. What I make happen for others, God will make happen for me. This is not only a spiritual principal found in the Word of God, but it also is a natural law that all of the physical world adheres to. No one plants or invests something of any kind without expecting to reap a future harvest.

I have gleaned many lessons from my multiple traumatic experiences. Most importantly, I know I cannot allow bitterness, resentment, or lack of forgiveness to remain in my heart toward the people who hurt me or took advantage of me. These individuals may have been very selfish or thoughtless, and may have no idea how badly they hurt me. However, what's done is done and cannot be undone. No one can go back and start all over again, even if he wants to. The milk has been spilled. The water has already gone over the dam. I recognize that I have absolutely no control over what other people do, but I *do* have full control over my *reaction* to what they do. Everyone will someday give an account to God for the things done while on earth. No one will be asked to account for what someone *else* did. We will answer only for our *own* actions. That is very sobering. I'm very glad I won't be responsible for the things someone else chose to do. I'll have a big enough job answering for the things *I* chose to do. I experience healing and restoration for myself when I pray regularly for others, especially for those who have hurt me, whether they did it intentionally or not. Taking vengeance upon someone is God's job, not mine. If I try to get even with someone, I only operate at the same level they are operating on. There's a much better way to do things. I am reminded that, "every time I throw dirt, I lose ground." If I try to discredit someone else, I actually hurt myself more than I hurt the other person. The only way I can effectively short-circuit a "root of bitterness" in my own heart, is by sincerely praying for God's blessing upon the people who hurt me, rather than fighting back. That is the way that Jesus responded to those who hurt Him.

Over the years, I have observed many people who, unfortunately, chose to stop and camp beside their experience of pain or grief, rather than move on with their lives. They prefer to continually reopen their painful wounds, by re-living the past tragedy in their mind, actively preserving and maintaining anger and bitterness in their heart, though whatever happened to them took place many years earlier. For all practical purposes, their lives ended at the point where their pain or grief occurred. They are no longer productive. How tragic for them, as well as for the Kingdom of God! They are still existing. They are still breathing, but *not really* living.

I fully recognize that things may not be going the way I prefer, but I do have control over my *attitude* about how things are going. If I refuse to forgive others their misdeeds, I become my *own* worst enemy, because I am never able to flush the pain from my mind and heart. Thus, I am unable to be freed from the ravages and bondage of bitterness. I recall the adage, "To err is human, but to forgive is Divine." That is the only way to complete healing. Only then can I be free from the curse of bitterness.

Certainly, I have experienced an uphill battle that has continued for far more years than I ever dreamed it would. However, I look back over those years with much thanksgiving and gratitude, as I recall what God taught me and accomplished in me because of my experiences. I have certainly learned a lot about myself. More importantly, I have learned a great deal about God. One thing is clear, I have learned that His grace and His faithfulness are much more than just something to sing about at church on Sunday mornings. He has taught me to see the good that He is able to produce out of apparent bad things. I have learned, first hand, that the "joy of the Lord" really *can* be my strength. It is a very *real* commodity. I have learned that God really *does* answer prayer. I have learned that the Word of God is relevant for me *today*. I have also learned that God sometimes answers my prayer by performing an absolutely glorious miracle. At other times, He responds by simply guiding me to select the best choice or action, so *I'm* involved in the solution or answer. Day by day, year after year, I have seen God continue leading me gently toward total restoration and healing in every area of my life.

> The wicked borroweth, and payeth not again; but the righteous showeth mercy, and giveth. Psalm 37:21

I am so glad I didn't follow the advice of many well-meaning friends who sincerely recommended I file bankruptcy. That appeared to them to be the most logical choice, economically, many years ago, as this would have hopefully given me a fresh start. I fully acknowledge that this would have been the easiest way out of my dilemma at the time, but I firmly believe that I made the decision God wanted me to make. He took me on a wilderness journey that lasted many years. Now I believe He is leading into His "Promised Land" of provision and blessing in every area of my life. The success of my real estate business relies heavily upon my reputation, integrity, and honesty, as observed and experienced by those I serve. I am convinced I have achieved more of these necessary traits by taking the route God led me to take. I can look each of my creditors in the eye, because they know I have done my best to pay them in full. I can also empathize much easier with clients I work with who have been, or are going, through tough times. Therefore, I can be of greater assistance to them as they work to get themselves onto more solid financial footing. I realize I have lost many things, especially material possessions, as well as fifteen or twenty years of my life. However, I have gained many other things that I consider to be of priceless value. These are the things I prefer to focus on. Furthermore, I believe I have found a spiritual depth, a root, and a focus in life I never would have found, if I hadn't gone through the tough times in my life. I am experiencing a ongoing series of marvelous miracles in my life. I am reminded that "it's not over 'till it's over." The struggles of my life have given me a greater appreciation for the many benefits and blessings God is giving me now. Therefore, I have determined to never take these things for granted again.

> *Brethren, I count not myself to have apprehended: but this one thing I do, forgetting those things which are behind, and reaching forth unto those things which are before, Philippians 3:13*

At the beginning of this book, I shared several of the very traumatic experiences that occurred in my life over a period of years. Lest I leave you wondering the ultimate outcome of these experiences, I want to relate to you God's provision and faithfulness. The rest of this book will deal with His marvelous restoration and glorious victory on my behalf. My experiences will illustrate that it's very important to keep on keeping on, to *never* give up on either God or yourself.

SEE WHAT GOD HAS DONE

The incidence of intense, severe pain in my lower abdomen, during a drive home from an out-of-town appointment, was soon diagnosed as a kidney stone. As I laid on the gurney in the emergency room, experiencing sharp, overwhelming pain, I was convinced I was dying. At that point, a nurse finally gave me a shot of morphine, and I was thankful someone had produced that specific drug. The pain soon lifted, and the doctor recommended I spend the night in the hospital for further observation. However, I refused. A night in the hospital would simply have increased the size of the pending bill, which already was larger than I cared to think about. I was sure I would rest just as comfortably at home, so they gave me a few painkillers to take along, in the event the pain recurred.

During the next couple of days, a number of friends joined with me in prayer for a miracle, and the urologist stood by to perform emergency surgery, if necessary. Since I wasn't covered by health insurance, I obviously resisted the thought of surgery, because of the several thousand dollars this would cost. The pain came back frequently, and then abated once I took another painkiller. A few days later, I was awakened early in the morning with another pain attack. This time, instead of taking a painkiller, I got up and sat in my recliner. During the next couple of hours, I quoted Scripture verses from memory, prayed, and sang songs of worship unto the Lord. I was amazed at how many Scriptures and songs I knew by heart, as the Holy Spirit brought them to my remembrance. Eventually the pain subsided, and I went back to bed. This incident occurred over three years ago, and the pain has never

---

returned. I continue to praise the Lord for His miraculous healing touch. Yes, God *is* still in the healing business today.

The story of Heidi, our registered Sheltie who disappeared during a flight of hot air balloons over our house, also has a happy ending. My daughter, Gretchen, and I quickly realized that we needed special help in finding her, as we were home alone. Together we knelt beside one of the big trees in our backyard and prayed that God would help us. Then we got up and went down toward the creek at the bottom of our half-acre backyard. We crossed it, and went up through the backyard of the home behind us. As we got up to the street in front of that home, we looked up the sidewalk and saw Heidi walking toward us. She responded quickly to our call, and within just minutes of our asking the Lord for His help, we had Heidi back in our house again. Yes, God is even concerned about a lost dog. We still had to make the effort to go find her, but He showed us which direction to go after we asked for His help.

A loving, Christian family adopted the baby son born to my single daughter. She selected them through an "open adoption" arrangement with a local Christian adoption agency. He is now being raised with another adopted brother, so he is part of a complete family. I shall never forget the special evening nearly a year after the adoption occurred, when my daughter was asked to be the featured speaker for the adoption agency's annual Thanksgiving banquet. She shared her emotional story with the group. Through prior arrangement, as a special finale to her speech, she was able to introduce her birth son and his new family to the audience. It was a thrill to meet his new parents for the first time, and to hug both my daughter's birth-son and his brother before we parted for the evening. That was the last time I've seen him, but I regularly pray that God will bless and use him in a very powerful way. My daughter cannot initiate any further contact with him until he is eighteen. She struggles occasionally with her feelings of loss and pain, but she is very encouraged by the letters and pictures she receives from his family, knowing that he is doing well. This outcome is another example of letting God provide His wisdom and strength to resolve a crisis dilemma, to achieve a happy ending.

I have visited with many other people who have experienced the trauma of divorce, but I have yet to encounter anyone who can quite match the drama of my experience in receiving God's healing power after a divorce. As evidence of that healing, I continue attending the same church that my ex-wife and her new husband attend. Neither of us chose to leave it after the divorce. It is a large church, and we both continue being involved in a number of ministries there. Thus, we see each other often at church, as well as at school or sports activities involving the kids.

A greater evidence of supernatural healing is that our relationship allowed a potentially difficult situation to be handled very successfully. Just over four years ago when they decided to purchase a new home, my ex-wife and her husband were comfortable enough with our relationship to ask me to represent them as their buyer's agent in the transaction. This was not an easy thing for either of us to accomplish. I am sure I struggled more with my emotions when they were

holding hands or hugging while we toured a number of prospective properties. However, the Lord helped me cope with my painful thoughts, and I was very grateful to be a part of their excellent purchase. I pray for them regularly and ask God's blessing upon their marriage. This prayer activity on their behalf has really made a major contribution toward helping me achieve the degree of personal healing and peace I've received since the divorce. I would have gained absolutely nothing by allowing myself to be unforgiving, angry or bitter over the way I was treated. I still have no good answer as to why divorce was the solution chosen for resolving our previous dilemma. However, it wasn't *my* choice, it was someone *else's*. I only have to account to God for the choices *I* make. I can't pretend that every interaction between us these days is a positive, wonderful experience, but I've observed that it is considerably better than most that I have observed in other people with similar situations.

So then every one of us shall give an account of himself to God. Romans 14:12

But I say unto you which hear, Love your enemies, do good to them which hate you, Bless them that curse you, and pray for them which despitefully use you. Be ye therefore merciful, as your Father also is merciful. Judge not, and ye shall not be judged: condemn not, and ye shal not be condemned: forgive, and ye shall be forgiven: Give, and it shall be given unto you; good measure, pressed down, and shaken together, and running over, shall

*men give unto your bosom. For with the
same measure that ye mete withal it shall
be measured to you again. Luke 6:27-28,
36-38*

*Say not, I will do to him as he hath done to
me...Proverbs 24:29*

The television ministry I helped establish in our city
continues to thrive and flourish. In 1998 we celebrated
twenty years of continuous ministry, twenty-four hours a
day, on our local cable channel. Several years ago, we
also added a UHF low-power station, so we can now
reach out 40 or 50 miles to the surrounding rural areas,
including many small-town cable systems. Technological
advances are continuing to expand our ability and
capacity to reach out even further through fiber optics,
and only God knows what the future holds for this
ministry. We are doing more and more local production,
and continuing to acquire better production equipment.
Thus, we are fully prepared to step through the doors of
opportunity as God opens them. I shake my head as I
vividly recall how much easier it would have been to
simply close everything down, admit defeat, and file
corporate bankruptcy on this fledgling ministry. However,
God provided the strength, the resources, and the right
people at the right time, continuing right up to the present
time. We still survive through regular miracles that God
performs to keep us going, but our financial books are
balanced. The struggle has certainly been an uphill one,
but the results have been well worth the price paid. Rapid
growth and expansion can put any business operation at
severe risk. We started with no contingency fund or plan.
Twenty years ago, when we started this ministry, I was

---

unaware of any book authored by someone who had successfully done this type of project. Thus I could not gain from someone else's experience. We had no track record to show a bank or potential donors to engage their assistance. There was also no one standing alongside with "deep pockets" to encourage and assist us in the nick of time with a welcome check. Therefore, it has been especially euphoric to simply observe what the Lord has done. A faithful few, committed people can still accomplish great things for the Lord, if they refuse to give up and refuse to lose their vision from the Lord. I continue serving on the board of KSCB, formerly called TEAM TV, and I praise the Lord that this ministry continues to be a viable part of our local community.

I have a very special memory from my tenure as acting President of TEAM TV. I was invited to Trinity Broadcasting Network in California. While there, I was interviewed as a special guest by Paul and Jan Crouch on their "Praise the Lord" national television program. It was such a privilege meeting them in person and personally observing this wonderful, successful Christian ministry in operation. That same evening during the telecast, the board and staff of TEAM TV conducted a dedication service for our new studio and office in Sioux Falls. I prayed the dedicatory prayer for that studio from the set of the TV studios during the interview at TBN. That program was broadcast live, via satellite, back to our offices in Sioux Falls. It was an awesome experience to actively participate in the modern miracle of television. I'll never forget it as long as I live. That was an experience I never dreamed I'd have, when I monotonously plowed the fields during those hot, muggy days as a kid on the farm.

I continue to miss my eldest son, Matthew, very much. Every so often I will have a flashback memory of him, especially when I see a guy in a cowboy hat, driving a black, extended-cab Chevrolet pickup. I often think about him when I am traveling down the interstate, or when I visit that same pizza restaurant with my other children, where he gave me his last big hug and told me that he loved me.

As another example of God's restoration, one of my daughters, Monique, recently married someone she met at Bible College. Interestingly, his name is Mathew, and he is the son of a Carpenter. They were married on July 10, 1999, which was the 26th birthday of my son, Matthew. A special tribute was made to him during the wedding. Thus, the Lord brought another Matt into my life, which helps soften the pain of the loss of my son. God does some incredible things to provide His resources, so we can cope with the problems of life. I continue to be thankful for the peace I have in my heart that my son Matt is in the presence of the Lord, and I am confident I will see him again when I get to Heaven.

I also thank God for how He has helped me deal with my real estate business. Mobility is a major concern in this business, since I usually have to show property in order to sell it. Nevertheless, I am happy to report that my records reveal that an average sale presently requires just two or three showings in order to for a sale to occur. I have sold several properties without *ever* showing them. I know very few Realtors could make a claim like that, so it is another way that the Lord has helped me cope with life until a physical miracle occurs, or something else develops. Some time ago, I decided to completely discontinue conducting Sunday open houses, because of the difficulty I had in standing for long periods of time. I also felt that God would be more pleased if I respected Sundays in a better way. Most Realtors consider Sunday open houses to be one of the main sources of their business activity. Nevertheless, my business activity has continued to increase and be strong without them. Responses to my ads, repeat business from past clients, and new prospects from personal referrals have continued to produce good sales activity. I made a sign that sits in front of my office desk. It is a slight variation of Psalm 127:1. It says, "Except the Lord sells the house, they labor in vain that sell it." The last few years, I have qualified for national top-producer awards for Coldwell Banker, the real estate franchise I represent as a broker-associate. Considering that I need to use a cane in order to stay mobile, I think the Lord certainly deserves the credit for this achievement.

I believe God can and will miraculously heal people today. Though I have earnestly sought His face and been prayed for by a great number of people, I don't know why my mobility limitation persists. However, it has become yet another opportunity for me to continue being optimistic, staying in good humor, and moving towards my goals, in spite of my physical circumstances. I would gain absolutely nothing by sitting around feeling sorry for myself, or by thinking God is mad at me for something. I know that is not the case, because He has been too good to me, and He loves me too much. Furthermore, only God can continue to give me the ability to hang on until I come out victoriously on the other side of this condition.

I am still walking with my cane, but the big news is that I *am still walking*. My general physical condition continues to require a miracle, before I can finally throw the cane away and walk without it. However, there is some improvement in my overall ability. At least my condition is no longer deteriorating. Climbing stairs remains a challenge, as does standing for long periods of time. Otherwise, I'm getting along well, even if I move a bit slower than I would like. I'd sure love to run again. I'd even settle for taking a brisk walk. In my heart, I continue holding a picture of myself walking. Often when I dream, I see myself walking without the cane, and I have recently done some limited walking without it. It would be particularly exciting to grab a tambourine and be able to dance across the platform at church some Sunday morning during the praise and worship portion of our service. In the meantime, I refer to myself as "the guy with the *cane* who is still *able*." The Lord has drawn my attention to a scripture verse found in Joshua 23:14 which has greatly encouraged me, especially since regaining my mobility is the last major area of restoration needing to happen in order to give me back everything the enemy has stolen from me. The verse says," And ye know in all your heart and in all your souls, that not one thing hath failed of all the good things which the Lord your God spake concerning you: all are come to pass unto you, and not one thing hath failed thereof."

HERE COMES THE BRIDE

The really big news, however, is something *most* unexpected that has happened. As a direct result of my lengthy seven-year involvement in authoring this book, I realized I needed to visit with someone who could give me expert advice on getting it from a rough, typewritten, draft stage, to publication. Through a series of interesting steps of faith, taken in obedience to the Holy Spirit's leading, I was directed to a wonderful, charming, beautiful, and talented woman named Joyce. We met indirectly through a mutual friend who owns a local Christian bookstore. One day I was attending a funeral and saw him standing next to me in the church foyer. I felt very impressed by the Holy Spirit to speak to him and ask if he knew anyone who could give me ideas on proper procedures for getting my book published. I had already typed the entire manuscript several times, and now needed to get it transferred to a computer for more effective editing. He said he didn't know of anyone offhand, but he'd give it some thought and get back to me. That same day, at the same funeral, he encountered another friend of his, Joyce, and during a brief conversation with her, discovered that she was in the process of completing her third book. The "light bulb" went on in his mind, and he called me that evening to suggest I call her for the needed assistance on my book.

I responded immediately and called her. We met a few days later so she could read my rough manuscript and offer some suggestions. While she read my manuscript, interspersed with asking many questions, I read one of her published books. However, something else took place that day that caught both of us totally off guard. During this initial meeting, we discovered we shared extremely similar backgrounds in nearly every area of our lives. Both of our mothers had been raised in or near the small town of White Lake, South Dakota. Our fathers were both farmers, and we had both grown up working with livestock and helping with the fieldwork on the farm. Both of us had been divorced from our former spouses, with neither of us wanting the divorces. Interestingly, both of us had also chosen to continue wearing our wedding rings for an *identical period* of three years after our divorces were finalized, hoping for eventual reconciliation with our former mates. However, we both ultimately realized that our hopes for reconciliation were in vain. We both had employment backgrounds as secondary education teachers, in the subjects of language arts and social studies, and had done graduate work beyond our college bachelor's degrees. We both drove white, four-door-cars, and lived in third-floor apartments. We both owned brass and glass tables, and had similar decorating tastes for our apartments. Most important of all, we both had definite personal experiences of salvation, a great love for the Bible, and vibrant, growing relationships with the Lord. We both were active in strong evangelical churches in our community. We shared a common interest in ministering God's healing and restoration power to other hurting people. All of this rapidly led to a mutual realization that the Lord was orchestrating something much more significant in our lives, more than just getting my book published.

A couple weeks later, I asked her if I could take her out for dinner, simply as an expression of my gratitude for her advice on my book. Initially, I wasn't sure I should even call it a date. I didn't know whether she was presently in a serious relationship with someone else, because we hadn't discussed that issue. However, she quickly agreed to go,

---

and we went to a local Italian restaurant. She wore a special blue dress she had purchased in Italy, while traveling in Europe the previous summer. As I opened the door for her at the restaurant, I commented that I needed to be careful so I "didn't fall for her." I was referring to my physical condition in walking with my cane, not wanting to lose my balance and fall in front of her, but obviously there was a double meaning *fully* intended. Our evening together was absolutely spectacular. After dinner, we went for a long drive in the country. By the time I took her home, we both knew we wanted to see each other again.

Almost simultaneously, a scripture verse which is found in Joel 2:25 became a very special verse to each of us. It says, "And I will *restore* to you the years that the locust hath eaten, the cankerworm, and the caterpillar..." We both felt God was speaking to us in a powerful way, promising total healing and restoration. The things that we had lost, or that had been stolen from us, would be returned or restored, all in God's time. Yes, God was up to something very good in our lives. A couple days later, my scheduled reading in the Bible for the day brought me to Proverbs 31, the chapter regarding the qualities of a good wife. This saga was continuing to get most interesting for both of us.

We had a total of seven dates over a fourteen-day period. It was a whirlwind courtship that dazzled us. However, it also produced a strong sense of the Lord's leading, with a mutual confidence and peace that we were in God's perfect will and timing. Joyce had been single after her divorce for ten years, and I had been single for seven following mine. Neither of us was sure we'd ever marry again, because we had come to the place where we had learned to be very content as singles. We had no interest in marrying again, unless we were fully convinced it was God's will. So many significant, astounding things took place in that short period of time, that all of our fears and concerns quickly vanished. We were reminded that the Lord promised to do a "quick work in the last day," but we never imagined it could also apply to a courtship. I kidded her once about our having a "barn-burner" relationship. Then she told me that, when she was a child, she accidentally started a fire in the barn on their farm. Fortunately, her mom had been able to extinguish the fire before it got out of control and burned the barn down. As far as our relationship was concerned, it seemed that God was adding more fuel to the fire, certainly not trying to put it out.

On our third time together, I took her to a cell group meeting at my church, where I had been asked to share my personal testimony regarding the importance of forgiveness and being free from bitterness. When I introduced her, I told the group this is what "an answer to prayer" looks like. As I sat beside her that evening and shared from my experience, I suddenly sensed the Holy Spirit speaking a strong message to my heart. He specifically told me He would show me how the great pain of my past would turn out to be the best thing that ever happened to me. Suddenly, I knew that, in spite of all the pain I had encountered, He had been faithfully working in my heart all along to prepare me for my best days, which were ahead of me, not behind. I always love it when I sense the Holy Spirit speaking something specific to my heart, but this particular message was unusually powerful, exciting, and thought-provoking, especially when it now appeared that Joyce was very likely to be a part of those future events.

One Saturday afternoon in February, just fourteen days after our first date, I took Joyce for a ride in the country. I told her I wanted to show her a very special place. I drove slowly along a winding, hilly country gravel road. As we approached a one-lane trestle bridge, which crosses the Sioux River on the border of Iowa and South Dakota, we were visiting and thoroughly enjoying each other's company. In the background, by my prior arrangement, a recording of songs from the movie, "The Preacher's Wife," sung by Whitney Houston, was playing on the stereo. I pulled onto the bridge and pushed the CD button for track eight, "You are Loved." We had watched this particular movie on our second date, so the song had a lot of significance. I stopped in the middle of the bridge and put my arms around her. Then I said, "On this bridge which represents crossing over from where we have been, our past, to where we are going, our future, I want you to know that I want you, I need you, I love you, and I am asking you to be my wife." I am delighted to report that she quickly responded in the affirmative. We sealed everything with lots of kisses. At this point, we had absolutely no idea just how significant this specific bridge was going to be to us in the near future.

During this time, I reflected on an experience that occurred the previous summer, prior to meeting and falling in love with Joyce. One day, upon entering my apartment in August of 1997, I sensed the Holy Spirit speaking clearly to my heart that I should remember the importance of the number *seven*. I immediately recalled that seven signifies the number of fulfillment or completion, and is used frequently by God in the Bible to speak messages to His people. After pondering this subject matter for a brief time, I suddenly recalled that it had been exactly seven years since my first wife had announced that she wanted out of our marriage, and had filed for divorce. As previously mentioned, I had also experienced a seven year period of time, prior to the divorce, when my former wife had refused to permit any kind of physical relationship between us. Now my memory of the significance of the number seven prompted me to do a brief, refresher Bible study about the subject and its importance to God's people. God seemed to be telling me that the period of drought (or life in the wilderness) was about to end for me. There also seemed to be something very significant that I needed to capture about the number seven. I realized that God was up to something really special in my life. I just needed to keep my eyes on Him, so I wouldn't miss His specific directions. God certainly had my attention at this point.

Following that experience, the Lord also stirred my heart about a related subject. This pertained to the year of jubilee, as mentioned in the Old Testament book of Leviticus, chapter twenty-five. That portion of Scripture describes God's plan for a time of healing and restoration to take place among His people every fifty years (seven X seven plus one). At that time, all possessions, which had been sold or mortgaged, would be restored to the original owners, and all debts would be cancelled. That way, everyone was given a fresh start in life every fifty years.

Furthermore, all slaves would be given their freedom. The nation of Israel celebrated the year of jubilee again in 1998, the first one since it became a separate nation in 1948. Many books were written and many messages were preached during 1998 about this exciting subject of jubilee, as there is great spiritual significance for Christians, as well as for the Nation of Israel. 1998, the year of jubilee, turned out to be the same year that I would meet and marry Joyce. I felt strongly in my heart, during 1997, that major changes were about to take place in *my* life, but I *never* dreamed that God's plans for me would include getting married again. It wasn't that I wasn't interested in the possibility. I usually spent a little time "scoping out the field" for potential candidates whenever I went to public gatherings. I would always ask the Lord to specifically speak to me, should there be someone there of whom I should take special notice. However, God gave me no specific inspiration on the subject, so I did very little dating. Furthermore, I wasn't sure I could ever trust someone again. I had long subscribed to the idea that I would much rather be single and wish I were married, than to be married and wish I were single.

After Joyce and I announced our engagement to shocked family and friends, we began making wedding plans. We selected May 30th for our wedding date. There seemed to be no logical reason to wait any longer to get married. We were both very confident of God's leading in our budding relationship. After we had completed all of the necessary wedding arrangements, I started kidding her that maybe we should just elope. The idea began to become more and more appealing to both of us. When we brought this unusual idea up to the pastor who was going to marry us, he responded very warmly to the possibility of having two weddings, and he offered to perform both of them. That is when we decided to get married on the same country-bridge where I had proposed to her.

Spring in South Dakota can be a bit unpredictable, but we selected the day before Easter, April 11th, 1998, for our "elopement" wedding. Because this was the day before Resurrection Day, we felt this was a very appropriate choice. We were looking forward to the beginning of a new life for both of us. We also realized, later, that Easter Sunday was exactly fifty days (seven X seven plus one) after our engagement took place. Thus, there was literally a "Day of Jubilee," a fresh start, occurring for us.

We wanted this wedding on the bridge to be very simple and private. For our marriage license, we went to a different county than the one we lived in. That way the legal notice wouldn't appear in our local newspaper and leak our secret. We also decided to continue keeping the date of May 30th reserved for a public wedding and reception, so our family and friends would be able to attend and share the event with us. When we looked at the calendar and started counting the days, we suddenly realized that our "bridge wedding" would take place exactly seven weeks after our engagement, and that our public wedding would be exactly fourteen weeks after our engagement. We were beginning to realize that God really does have an interesting sense of humor. Our first date had been on the seventh day of the month, and I had been inspired to purchase seven multi-colored roses for her on our second date, which was Valentine's Day. When we shopped for our wedding rings, we both decided we really liked a particular ring for her. Then we counted the stones and discovered that there were fourteen of them. This was starting to get really crazy, and we just knew we had to have that specific ring. To keep things consistent, we also knew that my ring would need to have seven stones. When the jeweler mailed the rings to us, we noted that the postage paid on the box was $7.77. It just seemed that, everywhere, we kept running into this reaffirmation of God's special message using the number seven, which confirmed to both of us His plan for completion, fulfillment and the year of jubilee, the time of new beginnings. God's message to me several months previously regarding the number seven or double seven was certainly making its impact upon us.

The day of our secret "bridge-wedding" turned out to be a wonderful, mild spring day. I got verbal permission from the county highway superintendent to briefly block the one-lane bridge during the wedding. We used my car as a backdrop for the ceremony, and tied fourteen balloons to the front bumper. We spread a roll of white plastic tablecloth on the roadway for Joyce's "carpet," so her full, white wedding gown wouldn't get dirty when she walked up the approach of the bridge to meet me. It was a bit windy that day, and we had to anchor the plastic with several small rocks we found nearby. By opening up the sunroof and all of the windows in my car, we were able to use the car's stereo system to play a cassette tape of the traditional wedding march, as professionally performed on a pipe organ. Joyce walked up the incline of the bridge approach on her unusual "white carpet" to meet me in our special "outdoor cathedral," as the sound of wedding music filled the river valley. She was absolutely radiant, as only a pure bride could be. We wrote our own wedding vows, which made the event even more special. We were concerned about the possibility of losing the wedding rings through the bridge floor spacing, and having them drop in the river, in case one of us nervously dropped a ring during the ceremony. That would not have been a humorous experience. To handle this dilemma, our pastor came up with the unique idea of tying the rings to fishing line secured to his belt. Once the rings were in place on the proper finger, we simply cut the line with a fingernail clipper. The ceremony was brief and simple, but this bridge wedding at the same site where our engagement was formalized, continues to bring much joy and pleasure to our hearts every time we recall the event. We return to this special spot frequently, to repeat our vows and revel again in our precious memories. After the wedding, we had a brief weekend honeymoon in the bridal suite of a local luxury hotel. We certainly experienced the beginning of restoration and healing from the Lord, something that will continue for the rest of our lives. (A year later, we celebrated our first anniversary in an unusual manner. Joyce put her wedding dress back on, and I put on my wedding suit and tie, and we went back to the bridge to repeat our vows and take pictures. Then we returned to the same bridal suite for the night. We love relishing our special memories.)

Most of the people who attended the public wedding on May 30th had no idea that there had already been a secret wedding on April 11th. After the "repeat ceremony" was completed, the pastor introduced us to the congregation as husband and wife. As previously planned, I took the microphone and began telling "our story," as several slides appeared on the big overhead screen. There were scenes from our brief, but exciting courtship. When slides of the "bridge-wedding" appeared on the screen, I expressed initial bewilderment about how those scenes could have gotten into the projector. After several more slides of the wedding appeared, I finally confirmed that we had already been married for seven weeks. We wanted everyone to know that we had gone ahead with the previously scheduled church wedding so we could still share the event with our friends and family. I asked them if they remembered the jingle, "Double your pleasure, double your fun, with Doublemint® chewing gum." As a special remembrance of our double wedding, double honeymoon, and double fun, we asked our ushers to give everyone a stick of Doublemint® gum as they were dismissed to go to the reception line. We had several people comment that this was the most special wedding they had ever attended. We had to agree with them.

We arranged for a limousine to pick us up after the reception and take us to our honeymoon suite. The chauffeur asked us if we had any special place we'd like to go first. We quickly responded that we'd like to go to "our bridge." She drove us there, and we had her take several pictures of us on the bridge with the decorated limousine. When we had the pictures developed later, we were absolutely amazed to find that the numbers on the license plate of the limousine equaled a double set of sevens.

We had a second honeymoon following the second wedding. We spent a week at a romantic, log cottage in the Black Hills of South Dakota. A babbling brook circled behind the cottage, which was surrounded by a ring of heavily-forested mountains. We had to look up to see out, which is a bit prophetic in itself. A hot tub graced the private rear deck overlooking the charming brook. This is where we spent many glorious hours of relaxation and bonding. We sang many songs of worship, and spent considerable time praying and reading the Bible together, thanking God for the marvelous work He had begun in our lives. Though it was the first week of June, we got a heavy snowfall one day, which really added another positive note to the atmosphere. It was an incredible experience to sit in a hot tub with the steam rolling around us as the snowflakes melted on our hair and faces. The solitude produced an environment that provides many special memories of the week. We determined that we wanted to return as often as possible to this special haven. Truly, 1988 turned out to be a "year of jubilee" from the Lord for both of us, a year of healing and restoration. As promised in Joel 2:25, The Lord is indeed restoring all of the things that had been previously stolen from us by our enemy, Satan.

A few months later, we determined that God was leading us to build a new log home in the country on the same farm where I had grown up. I never dreamed that I would ever return to the farm, especially to build a new home and live for the rest of my life. I thought I was a "city-slicker" for good. Nevertheless, the idea quickly gathered steam, and we moved forward rapidly. We credit part of the inspiration for building a log home to the experience of spending our memorable "second honeymoon" in the log cottage in the Black Hills of South Dakota. I designed the basic floor plan for this new home on our computer, using the features of this cottage as a basic format. After we made all of our plans and signed the building contracts, we realized that the site we had chosen for our new home was approximately seven miles, "as the crow flies," from "our bridge" where we were first married. We were approximately seven miles from the courthouse where we had gotten our marriage license. We also realized that we had driven past the site of our new home the evening of our first date, but little did we know, at that time, all the future would hold for us. We moved to the building site with a 30-foot travel trailer, so we could live next door during the construction. That same day we also realized that we were the seventh Swanson family currently living as neighbors in separate homes on the family farm property of approximately 900 acres. It is most appropriate that there will be a room in the loft area of this new house, which will be utilized as a prayer and meditation room, since God is certainly at the center of our marriage and our home. We call it the "Upper Room," and believe that many wonderful, powerful encounters with the Lord will occur there. The only window in the loft is a skylight, so it makes me feel just a bit like Noah did when he was on the ark. Our new phone number has a 743 prefix, which equals two sets of seven, and the last four digits contain numbers equaling two sevens. Our assigned 911 street address also has a double set of sevens in it. When we moved out of our condo apartment to our new home site, I realized that I had lived in the same condominium building for one month short of seven years. We have decided to name the driveway coming into our property from the highway "Jubilee Lane." A hand-carved, wooden sign will hang from the covered front porch declaring this home to be "Jubilee House." After all, this house will belong to God, and will stand as a testimony to His wonderful ability to heal and restore even the most complicated circumstances and losses in our lives. We intend to plant a blue spruce tree in our front yard, as a memorial dedicated to the memory of my son, Matthew, as this is the farm where he so loved to be every time he could.

There is so much more that I would like to be able to share about this "marriage made in Heaven," but I will simply say that God surely knows what He is doing when He begins moving in our lives. He has certainly demonstrated to Joyce and me that He is worthy of our complete trust and faith. I never dreamed when He began the work of healing and restoration in me, that He could accomplish such a superb work so quickly, especially because it seemed, at the time, that the years of heartache and pain were *never* going to end. Both Joyce and I are completely overwhelmed by all that He has already done to bring about healing and restoration in both of us, and we are convinced that He has just barely begun to do all that He has planned. Every morning when I awaken, I thank God for the presence of my sweetheart lying there beside me. We usually cuddle like a couple of kittens. The harmony, love and sense of purpose between us is absolutely awesome. Joyce is currently assisting me in the real estate business and doing some substitute teaching. Her latest book, *Exploding the Big Bang*, has been published, and we enjoy going together on book signing tours or activities promoting it in various churches. We are also involved in a number of activities relating to the creation/evolution issue, which promote creationism. We are making plans to begin hosting a local television program, which will air on our KSCB network in the near future. This is the same station I helped start over twenty years ago. We can hardly wait for each new day to arrive, so we can experience the great things God has in store for us.

In conclusion, I came across an interesting article some time go, regarding Ludwig von Beethoven. Anyone recognizing his name, will realize that this man was a premiere musician and composer. More than 150 years after his death, his music still inspires and entertains. His Ninth Symphony has been hailed by some as perhaps his finest work. This symphony is all instrumental music until near the end, when one single baritone voice begins chanting, "joy, joy…" Soon others join in until an entire chorus of voices was singing, "joy, joy…"

The first time the Ninth Symphony was ever performed, it generated such enthusiasm what when the "joy" section crescendoed, it was almost as though someone gave a command for the audience to rise to their feet and cheer. They applauded clamorously, but Beethoven did not even notice. Finally, one of the singers leaned over and tapped Beethoven on the shoulder to show him what the audience was doing. The reason that he had not heard the commotion was simple. *He was deaf.* In fact, at that point, he had been deaf for ten years.

Beethoven could have been content in his circumstances. After all, deafness for any musician, especially one the caliber of Beethoven, would be extremely trying. He could easily have said that he was going to wait for more favorable circumstances in order to write about and exercise joy, but he didn't. Instead, even in the midst of what was seemingly the very worst that life had to offer him, he chose to be active, viable, and creative. Like the Apostle Paul wrote in Philippians 4:12, "I have learned the secret of contentment no matter what state I am in." Nothing else but our relationship with the Lord will bring lasting contentment to us. Nothing else in all of life is able to give us that extra special ability to rise above our circumstances and to achieve dreams that seem totally impossible to the ordinary person.

In that same spirit, I have continued to pursue my dreams diligently. Furthermore, I am delighted to report that I am continually finding more and more things for which to be thankful. Life is more exciting than it has ever been, and I have experienced many miracles on a regular basis in my business, as well as in my personal life. God is showing me that it is a whole lot more fun, as well as more productive, to be a giver, rather than a taker. I am happy to be able to report that there *is* life after divorce. There *is* life after the death of a loved-one. There *is* life after experiencing major physical problems. There *is* life after experiencing devastating financial problems. There *is* life after raising your children. There *is* life after leaving one church for another. There *is* life after embarrassing, personal failure and having dreams and goals of life dashed. The only way to fully experience these victories is to *never, never, never* give up. The final chapter of my life has not been written yet. It's not over 'till it's over.

I recall a statement I heard recently, which originated with a pastor. Over the years, he had been present during the death experience of a great number of people. His published report was he never overheard anyone, in any of those experiences, indicate that he wished he had spent more time at the office during his life. Rather, many other things were mentioned that should have been done during life, while there was still opportunity. If that would hold true for us as well, why is spending more time at the office, or at any other activity, so high on our list of priorities? I remember seeing a plaque in our home when I was growing up. It said, "Only one life, 'twill soon be passed. Only what's done for Christ will last."

> *For I know the plans I have for you, saith the Lord, and they are plans for good and not for evil, plans to give you a hope and a future...Jeremiah 29:11*

Yes, life and people can definitely be cruel at times, but God is for real. God still cares about everything that happens to us. Even when it appears we are losing everything in life that we care about or hold dear to our hearts, we need never lose our faith, our joy, or our ability to persevere in spite of the crisis. We needn't lose the ability to experience, once again, someday very soon, the goodness and blessing of the Lord in our lives. When nothing seems to make any sense, when fear and dismay pierce our heart and soul, when all hope appears to be gone, we must not forget that *God is still on the throne. God is still bigger than Satan. God still knows how to help us. God still loves us. God loves to make a way where there doesn't appear to be one. He loves to open doors that no one else can open.* We will be able to smile and laugh again, even if that doesn't appear to be the remotest possibility at this point.

Blessed are ye that weep now: for ye shall laugh Luke 6:21b

Finally, brethren, whatsoever things are true, whatsoever things are honest, whatsoever things are just, whatsoever things are pure, whatsoever things are lovely, whatsoever things are of good report: if there be any virtue, and if there be any praise, think on these things. Philippians 4:8

I want to share a couple more of my favorite great songs of faith with you.

TO GOD BE THE GLORY
Fanny J. Crosby/ William H. Doane (public domain)

To God be the glory, great things He hath done.
So loved He the world that He gave us His Son,
who yielded His life, an atonement for sin,
And opened the Life gate, that all may go in.

O perfect redemption, the purchase of blood,
To every believer the promise of God!
The vilest offender, who truly believes,
That moment from Jesus a pardon receives.

Great things He hath taught us, great things

He hath done.
And great our rejoicing, through Jesus, the Son;
But purer, and higher, and greater will be,
Our wonder, our transport, when Jesus we see.

Chorus—
Praise the Lord. Praise the Lord.
Let the earth hear His voice.
Praise the Lord. Praise the Lord.
Let the people rejoice.
Oh, come to the Father, through Jesus the Son,
And give Him the glory, great things He hath done.

This song has special meaning because it was sung at my mom's funeral, and I continue to sing it on occasion. The song briefly sums up much of my personal testimony in just three verses.

THROUGH IT ALL
Andrae Crouch, copyright 1971
Manna Music, Inc.

I've had many tears and struggles.
I've had questions for tomorrow.
There've been times I didn't know right from wrong.
But in ev'ry situation, God gave blessed consolation
That my trials only come to make me strong.

I've been to lots of places,
And I've seen a lot of faces,
There've been times I felt so all alone.
But in my lonely hours, yes, those precious
lonely hours,
Jesus let me know that I was His own.

I thank God for the mountains
And I thank Him for the valleys,
I thank Him for the storms He brought me
through.
For if I'd never had a problem,
I wouldn't know that He could solve them,
I'd never know what faith in God could do.

Chorus—
Through it all, through it all,
I've learned to trust in Jesus,
I've learned to trust in God.
Through it all, through it all,
I've learned to depend upon His Word.

These are a couple of favorite poems of mine, which are most appropriate to share as a conclusion:

DON'T QUIT   **Edgar A.Guest**

When things go wrong, as they sometimes will.
When the road you are trudging seems all up hill.
When the funds are low and the debts are high,
And you want to smile, but you have to sigh.
When care is pressing you down a bit,
Rest, if you must, but don't you quit.

Life is queer with its twists and turns,
As every one of us sometimes learns,
And many a failure turns about
When he might have won had he stuck it out.
Don't give up, though the pace seems slow.
You might succeed with another blow.

Success is failure turned inside out –
The silver tint of the clouds of doubt.
And you can never tell how close you are,
It might be near when it seems afar.
So stick to the fight when you are hardest hit.
It's when things get worse that you mustn't quit.

GOD HATH NOT PROMISED

God hath not promised skies always blue,
Flower strewn pathways all our lives through.
God hath not promised sun without rain,
Joy without sorrow, peace without pain.
But God has promised strength for the day.
Rest for the laborer; light on the way.
Grace for the trial, help from above,
Unfailing sympathy – undying love. (author unknown)

Remember,
a winner never quits
and a quitter never wins!

INDEX OFSONGS

Roger Swanson is available
for public speaking engagements.
For more information,
contact him at Masterpiece Creations,
(605)743-5972.